New Evidence
for the
Middle School

Paul S. George
Kathy Shewey

NATIONAL MIDDLE SCHOOL ASSOCIATION

nmsa ®

NATIONAL MIDDLE SCHOOL ASSOCIATION

Paul George has long been an internationally recognized leader in the middle school movement. A professor at the University of Florida in Gainesville, Dr. George has authored four previous NMSA monographs. Kathy Shewey is a veteran middle school teacher, team leader, and active professional. Since 1989 she has been a consultant for the National Resource Center for Middle Grades/High School Education. The National Middle School Association is grateful for the volunteer service of these educators in preparing, conducting, and reporting on this valuable study.

ISBN 1-56090-084-9

Contents

N *ew Evidence for the Middle School.* The title itself excites. How eagerly have educators caught up in this major educational movement sought positive evidence. And while this monograph is certainly not the last word, and the authors carefully make no such claim, it is an important and encouraging publication. The information and data presented here will help to fill the frequently noted research void in the middle school movement. There has been a tremendous, enthusiastic, and often impassioned voice promoting middle schools in the last thirty years. That advocacy, however, has often been turned aside because of the lack of sufficient research evidence to validate the practices proposed. A gut-level certainty that they were on sound ground sustained the already converted advocates, but it often was insufficient to persuade boards of education and others—although no research could be cited to justify the continuation of present practices.

Studies done in the 60s and 70s which sought to compare middle schools with junior high schools were ineffective. These survey studies seldom touched the real programmatic factors, assumed differences based on school title or grade organization, and, not surprisingly, produced inconclusive and disappointing results.

To provide the evidence needed to change school practices, it was evident that a different type of educational research was needed. Such an approach emerged under the name *outlier studies.* Research studies using this approach have had an impact on middle school education. Most of the studies reported here used this new approach to educational research.

In Part One the authors provide an excellent overview of early research activities in middle level education and describe the outlier research thrust. They then detail the results of several studies which yielded substantial evidence to support the efficacy of the middle school concept.

In Part Two the 1985 study of 130 middle schools which had been deemed particularly successful or exemplary is described and its results are detailed. These schools rather uniformly evidenced a number of common characteristics, the very characteristics which have received consensus endorsement as central to the middle school concept. While the authors are cautious in generalizing, the results, nevertheless, were very encouraging. Middle level schools that had been judged by others as outstanding in 1985 displayed a consistent and almost universal incidence of team organization, teacher-based guidance activities, flexible use of time, faculty participation in decision-making, and other tenets of the middle school concept. And highly positive results in academic achievement, school climate, faculty morale, student behavior, and other factors were evident as well.

The 1993 study conducted by the authors is described in Part Three. Comprehensive reports from 108 schools were analyzed to reveal the presence of and the effectiveness of middle school components that are widely recommended for schools serving 10-15 year olds. Both objective and subjective data are presented. Although the 1993 sample was not as selective as the 1985 sample, these new data are now a part of the mounting body of evidence that demonstrates those schools which implement the middle school concept are achieving measurable success.

—John H. Lounsbury

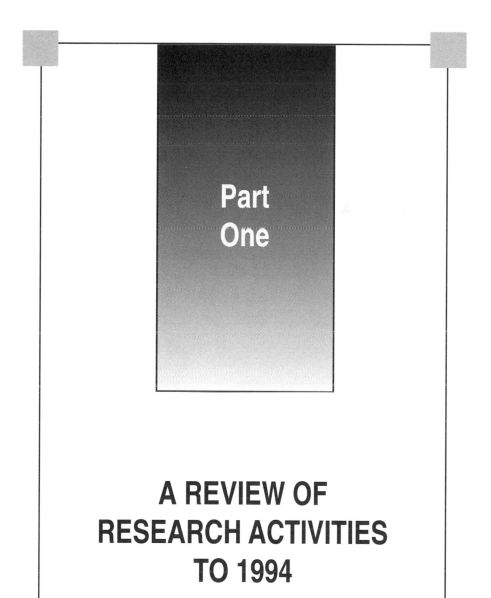

**Part
One**

A REVIEW OF
RESEARCH ACTIVITIES
TO 1994

As the 21st century looms on the horizon, the middle school movement remains the largest and most comprehensive effort at organizational and curricular change in the history of American public schooling. The contemporary middle school movement, by 1994, is at least 30 years old, and shows no sign of slowing. Hundreds of school districts, now perhaps thousands, in all fifty states and many other nations, have moved toward the middle school plan. The reorganization to middle schools, it seems certain, will continue unabated into the next century. Each year, dozens of school districts open newly reorganized middle schools as alternatives to K-8, 7-9, 7-12, or other pre-existing plans. In spite of a decline in the overall number of all types of schools in America as a result of decreasing enrollments, the number of identified middle schools continues to increase. Market Data Retrieval, Inc. reports that in 1992-93 there were 11,215 middle level schools as follows:

5 - 8 — 1,223		7 - 8 — 2,412	
6 - 8 — 6,155		7 - 9 — 1,425	

With other configurations (6 - 7, 6 - 9, single grade schools, etc.) the total exceeds 12,000 (C.K. McEwin, personal correspondence, May 21, 1994).

New efforts in the reorganization of middle level education are not restricted to the United States. Dozens of middle schools are now available to students in Canada, the United Kingdom, and in many international schools in Europe, South America, and Asia. Japan has become increasingly dissatisfied with the junior high school program and continues to implement components of the American middle school, especially those which relate to the recognition and support of students as individuals. China also offers what are called middle schools. Early adolescent education is an increasingly international concern.

> " **Early adolescent education is an increasingly international concern.**

For most of the last three decades, research reports on the effectiveness of middle school education have been inconclusive; confusing language and research design difficulties have introduced a considerable degree of misunderstanding into the discussions of middle school effectiveness at local, state, and national levels. Often, middle schools in name only have been compared with other middle level organizations, with the predictable lack of significant results as the outcome of dozens of studies. Consequently, educators, policy makers, and citizens are left without sufficient reliable information about whether such schools work better than the school organizations they replaced.

Beginning in the mid-sixties, middle schools often appeared in many districts as an educational expediency resulting from court-ordered desegregation, declining enrollments, or some other need not exclusively related to the education of young adolescents. For almost two decades, therefore, middle schools lacked adequate definition. But by the 1980s, educators began to arrive at a relatively complete consensus on the characteristics of successful middle schools. Many educators (Epstein, 1990; Mac Iver, 1990) with experience in middle level schools for older children and young adolescents now strongly endorse several common elements:

- ❏ classroom-based guidance efforts, often in the form of what have come to be called advisory programs;
- ❏ interdisciplinary team organization;
- ❏ common planning time for the team of teachers;
- ❏ flexible scheduling, often in a block format;
- ❏ a curriculum emphasizing balanced exploration and solid academics; arrangements which permit the development of longer-term relationships between teachers and the students they teach;
- ❏ heterogeneous grouping whenever appropriate;
- ❏ instructional strategies that consider the characteristics of the learner;
- ❏ a wide range of special interest experiences keyed to the development of middle school youth; and
- ❏ collaboration between and among teachers and administrators as they work to improve middle school programs (George and Alexander, 1993).

There is evidence to suggest that such program components are finding their way into more and more middle schools regardless of the name of the school or the grade levels included (Alexander and McEwin, 1989); yet there is, even in the 90s, less evidence on the effectiveness of such components in middle level schools than educators and community members desire.

This situation, although far from satisfactory, has improved significantly since the predecessor of this monograph (George & Oldaker, 1985) was published. The modern middle school movement enters its fourth decade, and has reached such magnitude that it is unequalled by any other national educational effort, save the century-long school consolidation movement. The National Middle School Association has assumed a new level of prominence among educational groups, attract-ing more than 10,000 people to its annual conferences. State and re-gional middle school associations in Florida, California, New England, Texas, North Carolina, and many other states, find themselves solidly established and able to wield substantial influence within their bor-ders. Articles asking whether the middle school is a fad no longer appear. School administrators, curriculum planners, university profes-sors, parents and bureaucrats at all levels recognize, and few challenge, the basic components of the middle school. Indeed, debates no longer focus on the desirability of teaming or other components of the middle school concept, save perhaps the advisory programs. The issue of which grade levels belong in the middle school, or the correct name of such schools, are no longer thought to be the most important concerns in the outcomes for students. There are, perhaps, as many as 25 million stu-dents being educated in today's American middle level schools and massive changes in these schools have been occurring for more than three decades, leaving virtually no American untouched. In 1994, America seems content with the middle school concept, even if not completely satisfied with the outcomes that have been achieved (Council of Chief State School Officers, 1992).

> **66**
> **America seems content with the middle school concept, even if not completely satisfied with the out-comes that have been achieved.**

School board members and parent groups considering new middle school programs continue to seek evidence that will support their reor-ganization effort, and turn to those with experience in middle schools. The accumulation of such evidence has been agonizingly slow, but steady. It is, however, not the first time major innovations have occurred in American education without little research support. In fact, as most educators know, the history of innovation in our schools is replete with instances of changes which came about, on a major scale, for every reason except that there was research evidence available for whatever was proposed. One example should be sufficient.

About thirty years ago, the first open space school buildings made their appearance. In a very short time, hundreds of new open space schools were designed, constructed, and opened all across the land. In an equally short time, teachers and parents reacted extremely negatively; soon portable walls were erected, followed by permanent walls in a year or two. Thirty years later, there are virtually no open space schools being built and the once wide-open spaces are nothing more than cramped versions of traditional classrooms. Many such schools have been completely remodeled.

After all of this, what do we know about the effectiveness of open space schools? What did research tell us? Virtually nothing. After reviewing almost 200 research studies of open space schools, one reviewer concluded that most of the research was so flawed that we learned nothing from it (George, 1975).

The predominant pattern of research on open space schools was, of course, a comparison of open space schools with traditional school buildings, and the predominant result was a report of no significant differences. It is likely that most open space schools never really operated as they were intended; individualized instruction and real team teaching did not appear the way designers had planned. Many open space schools ended up, therefore, containing exactly the same style of instruction, grouping and self-contained classes that were present in the traditional schools. Hence, many research studies compared two building designs that housed the same type of programs, with the expected results: no significant difference.

It might be argued that the open space school phenomenon was a fad that lasted about twenty years, touched many districts, affected the lives of many students and then faded away. The reasonable extension of that argument to the middle school, for some, might lead to a prediction of a similar end for the middle school movement. In 1994, happily, this seems less and less likely to occur.

RESEARCH PRIOR TO 1985 : OUTLIER STUDIES

Fortunately for the middle school, and for the advocates of that program, the middle school movement emerged during a propitious period in the history of educational research. In the previous decade, substantial progress had been made in the conduct of educational research; a point of maturity had been reached. Instead of making specious comparisons of subjects that cannot be reasonably compared, or conducting experiments in situations where experimental research has no place, researchers developed a new degree of skill in seeking the answers to important questions. This new sophistication in social science research emerged at just about the same time as the middle school was born.

Almost 30 years ago, James Coleman (1966) published a national study that focused on equal educational opportunity. After amassing mountains of data about student achievement, this influential study concluded that the only really significant factor in academic achievement was the socioeconomic status of the children who attended a school. The "home effect," as it came to be called, appeared to outweigh anything that educators attempted to do, and the implication was that teachers did not matter, that schools made no difference in the lives of the students who attended. Race and socioeconomic status were, it was implied, the determining factors in academic achievement; the "school effect" was unimportant and inconsequential.

Charges that teachers were inconsequential and that schools made no difference in the lives of children were, to educators, almost as infuriating as the implication that the children of the poor could not learn. Twenty years later, landmark research in what has come to be called "teacher and school effectiveness" was being eagerly consumed in virtually every school district and college of education in the country. This effectiveness research demonstrated, quite clearly, that teachers do make a difference and that poor children can learn well (Slavin, 1989). Major efforts at school improvement, based on this research, were undertaken in hundreds of districts, and student achievement scores responded positively.

These successful research efforts came to be known among researchers as "outlier studies." The term "outlier study" referred to research focused on the careful scrutiny of the most successful examples of a subject that could be found, those that lay outside the boundaries of the mediocre. Outlier studies concentrated on attempting to learn what makes the best become the best. In corporate life, the outlier research focused on corporations that managed to remain highly productive and profitable over long periods of time (Peters and Waterman, 1982). In education, it became the search for and study of the most successful teachers and the barrier-breaking schools.

This research followed several basic steps. First, researchers rejected the claim that there are no differences between teachers or schools. They began with the assumption that teachers can make a difference and that schools do matter. Second, they sought examples of teachers and schools who could be demonstrated to have made significant differences in the lives of students; they identified classrooms and schools where students made gains that went far beyond what could have been predicted or expected. Third, these exceptional teachers and schools became points of discovery, not of experiment. That is, researchers went to the classrooms and the schools where the successes were documented and attempted to discover what made the difference. Fourth, having discovered and described the characteristics of effectiveness in separate classrooms and schools, researchers then compared what they discovered about successful teachers to see what they might have in common. They examined the characteristics of successful schools to learn whether such schools have important similarities that could be linked to improved academic achievement. Finally, the researchers have attempted to develop models that can be used in assisting other teachers and schools to become more successful.

Instead of pursuing laboratory experiments, educational researchers had gone into the field to discover what worked well. Theory emerged from the discoveries, not the reverse. As a result, educators were much more able to identify which teacher behaviors were likely to be correlated with increased academic achievement and which characteristics of successful schools are common among the schools that make really positive differences in the lives of their students. Summaries of the results of the research on teacher and school effectiveness are available in a number of sources (Rosenshine & Stevens, 1986).

In the early 1980s, the pursuit of outlier studies as measures of school effectiveness was extended into the area of middle school education. Based on the assumption that schools did make a difference in the lives of their students, and that the degree and type of differences could be traced to the characteristics of the schools in question, educational researchers uncovered some important findings. Following the general guidelines for outlier studies, a number of different researchers, in quite different settings and for very different purposes, pursued their studies in quite similar fashion. Accepting the argument that grade level and name of the school were unlikely to be the cause for any significant differences among schools, oversimplified and specious comparisons of middle and junior high schools ceased to be the major focus. Much less time was spent on further attempts to determine which combination of grade levels holds the secret to success with early adolescents.

Research in the late 70s and the early 80s, instead, focused on the identification of schools that had an outstanding record of success which could be demonstrated to be free of dependence on the socioeconomic status or ethnic backgrounds of the students attending the school. Typically, an outstanding record of success was established by determining that the schools measured up to a number of important criteria for success (Lipsitz, 1984; Rutter, 1979). These factors included academic achievement scores on standardized tests, attendance rates, behavior in school, behavior out of school (i e , delinquency), parental satisfaction, and reputations for excellence at the local, state, or even the national level. Once these criteria had been satisfied, the schools became the subjects of intensive in-depth investigation.

During this period of the late 70s and early 80s, the emphasis among educators restructuring middle level schools turned to the area of school organization. After disappointing attempts to revitalize the curriculum and the instructional strategies of newly organized middle schools, educators began to focus on the theme of changing how students and teachers were organized to teach and learn together. This new awareness of the importance of school organization among middle school educators made the research in school effectiveness clearly relevant to the concerns of those educators.

The Rutter Study

One of the first such studies was conducted by Rutter and his associates (1979) in twelve junior high schools in inner-city London. When the study was published, it became well-known and discussed in detail in almost all of the reports of research on school effectiveness. It was significant for persons interested in middle level education because of the rigor of the research design and the fact that the findings provided an exciting confirmation of some of the central components of the middle school concept, in spite of the fact that they were discovered in junior high school settings.

Rutter discovered that within this sample of twelve junior high schools, several of the schools were very successful while others were not. Successful outcomes were not a matter of grade level or school name, obviously, since all twelve schools had the same name and grade levels. Nor were the successful schools identified by their physical or administrative features, the socioeconomic background of the students, or the differences in the elementary schools which fed the junior highs. The reasons for the success of some of the schools and the failure of others in this study appeared to be related to two different but closely related sets of factors: academic emphasis and the psychosocial environment.

As had been the case, generally, in the area of research on teacher and school effectiveness, the Rutter study confirmed the importance of an academic emphasis. Reasonably high expectations, direct instruction, homework, and other related items combined to enable teachers and students to take learning seriously and, as a result, to become more successful in mastering the learning tasks. In addition to this academic emphasis, however, Rutter and his colleagues concluded that the really crucial differences between the successful and unsuccessful schools in the study were in the area of the psychosocial environment, in the life of the school as a social organization.

> **...the really crucial differences between the successful and unsuccessful schools in the study were in the area of the psychosocial environment, in the life of the school as a social organization.**

A positive psychosocial environment was, the authors concluded, the enabling force which permitted teachers to be successful with the academic emphasis in the first place. The academically successful schools were those where the teachers and the students were able to see themselves as part of the same group, as members of the same team. Teachers and students, in the schools that reached beyond the expectations or predicted levels of achievement and behavior, shared the same educational perspective, the same norms for the life of the school.

Most important, insofar as the middle school was concerned, was that all of the factors that led to the "ethos of caring" characteristic of the successful schools are part and parcel of the American middle school concept in the 90s. Teachers working together, planning jointly, to establish conditions for students, promoting increased responsibilities and participation of students, establishing stable teaching and friend-ship groups that last for more than one year—all of these factors lay close to the heart of the middle school movement. Rutter understood, and made clear, the insignificance of the concerns for the name of the school, the grade levels included, or other factors which have been mistakenly perceived as important to the middle school by those new or uniformed about the process of middle level education (George, 1983, p. 71).

Rutter concluded, after four years of study, that the crucial differ-ences in the schools boiled down to whether or not the school effec-tively attended to the social side of learning. It was critically impor-tant, said Rutter, that teachers and students came to see themselves as part of the same school group, the same team. This unity permitted faculty and students to work together for common purposes in and out-side the classroom. Unity is what made it more likely that students shared the educational perspective of the faculty, and what, therefore, led ultimately to higher academic achievement.

The Phi Delta Kappa Study

Not too long after the Rutter study became known, Phi Delta Kappa published its own outlier study of the characteristics of schools that had what that association called *good discipline.* Over 500 schools responded to a detailed questionnaire that helped to establish the common characteristics of schools known for good student behavior. Among the recommendations that emerged from the study were several that middle school advocates claimed as central to that approach to the education of early adolescents (Phi Delta Kappa, 1982).

❑ Schools should find ways to improve how people in the school work together to solve problems.

❑ Schools should develop the means to reduce authority and status differences among all persons in the school.

❑ Schools should increase and widen the students' sense of belonging in the school.

❑ Schools should find a way to deal with the personal problems that affect life within the school. Programs called "advisor-advisee" were advocated.

❑ Schools should improve the physical and organizational arrangements so that these factors reinforced other efforts.

It is very easy to see in the above studies, from the perspective of the 90s, a clear if unarticulated reference to organizational approaches of the middle school such as the interdisciplinary team, the advisory program, and arrangements such as multiage grouping that permit strongly positive relationships, once established, to endure for more than one academic year. It appeared that distinctions which sharply separated concepts of curriculum and instruction from those of school organization were now obsolete; school organization was as much a part of the curriculum as the courses of study presented to students.

University of Florida Studies

Further support for this perspective on the centrality of school organization to the middle school concept emerged that same year in an important study at the University of Florida (Damico, 1982). A group of social psychologists and sociologists, concerned about how middle school organization might affect interracial contact among early adolescents, examined student interaction in six different middle level schools in the same school district. The schools had the same grade levels, the same designation (middle) and were attended by students from similar ethnic and socioeconomic backgrounds. The curriculum was the same in each school, established by curriculum committees and identical textbooks at the school district level. Everything about the schools was as similar as it could be, except for the ways in which the schools were organized.

Two of the six schools were organized as the middle school concept suggests, with interdisciplinary team organization, advisory groups, and multiage grouping which permitted teachers and students to stay together on the same team for three years. The other four schools had academic departments without teams, no advisory program and were organized so that teachers and students changed every academic year, with students being reorganized into new class groups each year. Because advisory programs and multiage grouping are, in several ways, components of the team organization, the real difference between the two groups of schools was that two schools had complete, fully-functioning teams and the others had no team organization at all.

Researchers concluded, after extensive examination of the interracial interaction in the schools, that the schools with the interdisciplinary team organization had a much more positive interracial climate. Students in these teamed schools had far more cross-race interactions, and these interactions resulted in significantly more positive perceptions of students of other races. Black students in the teamed schools saw school as being significantly better than did black students in the non-teamed schools. Students in teamed schools had more friends of other races and reported that the school was better and friendlier. Even in situations that could be observed, such as seating in the cafeteria and assemblies, there was much more voluntary cross racial seating. In the teamed schools, white students evaluated black students more positively, perceived interracial classroom climates more positively, and believed that interracial relationships, in general, were more positive than did white students in the non-teamed schools. It seemed clear that the team organization, with the advisory group program and multiage grouping, contributed significantly to the improvement of race relationships among young adolescents.

> **...the team organization, with the advisory group program and multiage grouping, contributed significantly to the improvement of race relationships among young adolescents.**

As an extension of this study of student perspectives of interracial relationships, Doda (1984) pursued an ethnographic analysis of two of the schools, one with the middle school concept, one without. Observing and analyzing several teachers in each of the two schools throughout the length of a school year, Doda discovered that teachers' perspectives and practices were "markedly different and that these differences were associated with the organization, curriculum and administration of the two schools" (Doda, vi).

At the middle school, teachers saw their role as an exalted one, difficult but terribly important. At the other school, however, teachers lacked these convictions, tending to view teaching as a burdened semi-profession with little opportunity to shape students' lives or futures. At the middle school, teachers saw themselves as responsible for helping students in a multitude of ways, whereas teachers at the second school saw themselves almost exclusively as disseminators of subject matter. These disparate goals and priorities found expression in the manner and style of classroom instruction and management.

While it was premature to attempt to assign causality, it seemed equally unwise to assume that school organization had no affect on teacher perspective or behavior. Doda argued that the team organization prompted a different perspective on the part of the middle school teachers she studied. These teachers valued each other, looked to one another for support and assistance, and talked of the educational process as a collective effort. At the other school, where no team organization existed, the teachers had significantly less contact with one another, and the contact that did occur was often brief and rarely task-related. In an earlier description of this activity, Doda described it this way (1982, p. 10):

> Life as a team member contributes to the middle school teacher's world view. It provides frequent teacher contact, opportunities to discuss the students that teachers have in common and it allows experimentation and the testing of new ideas. The team provides its teachers with camaraderie, support and friendship. Teachers view themselves as part of a collective which mitigates the burden of individual failure while bolstering professional self-esteem. Perhaps most important, the team is a decision-making unit. Teachers must make decisions collectively and must continually share ideas, attitudes, beliefs, views, and feelings. It may be this continual dialogue among teachers that promotes the teachers' view that their work is

significant. Moreover, the challenge of joint decision-making may provide a sense of power and control not found in the isolated teaching experience typical in the junior high school.

Working in the junior high's structure provided little or no opportunity for camaraderie or affiliation with a collective identity. Teachers spent most of their time alone and shared very few dimensions of school life with fellow colleagues. The burden of failure was largely an individual matter. The range of decisions made by the department was limited to that of curriculum and teachers generally did not discuss beliefs and ideas at length. The department serviced efficiency and did not encourage teacher interaction. Moreover, the department was not seen as a unit involved in school decision-making. While department chairpersons did meet from time to time with the administration, those meetings did not deal with school philosophy and policy. The department chairpersons were spokespersons for the department's curriculum concerns and there was seldom an opportunity for discussion of other school matters. Department membership did not require extensive involvement and participation. What teachers held in common was the curriculum, and individuals could execute the same curriculum with little dialogue between fellow members. The tasks they performed could best be done alone. This may account for the individualistic orientation that prevails at the junior high and perhaps simultaneously reinforces the focus on procedures over people.

One of the least known features of some exemplary middle schools, multiage grouping, permitted teachers and students to stay together on the same team for more than one year. In her study, Doda identified this feature as having particular significance in its impact on teacher perspectives and practices (1982, p. 13-14):

> Contrasting teacher emphases on students in the middle school and curriculum in the junior high may be more related to multiage grouping than to any other single difference. At the middle school teachers had the same students for three years. They viewed the three year experience as the most satisfying part of their job because it allowed them to see students grow and change over time. In three years, growth is generally dramatic in all areas of development. Perhaps teachers have a better chance of feeling exalted about their work and maintaining their focus on student development when they teach youngsters for an extended time and can witness this dramatic growth. For the teachers at the junior high who only have students for one year, student and teacher achievement are less obvious. Teachers' focus on short term results in curriculum mastery and test grades. Chances are that the teachers only glean that sense of heroic pride when a student returns years later for a visit. The entire staff at the middle school took an interest in making school enjoyable for students, while the staff at the junior high did not. No doubt, teachers' notions of students' improbability account for this, in part. However, the multiage grouping and teacher-student guidance program in the middle school resulted in teachers spending more time with students outside of the classroom.

This produced a focus on teacher-student relationships and in those relationships teachers were faced with students' honest feelings about school and learning. Recognition that school wasn't much fun for most students seemed to be a part of teachers' concerted efforts to make it otherwise. The indifference of teachers in the junior high regarding their responsibility for generating student enthusiasm could be explained by their infrequent opportunities to schedule fun into the school day. There were very few times during a school year when classes were suspended for a special student event. This was not so at the middle school. In addition, teachers did not have as much contact with students in a nonacademic setting. The teacher-student relationships were preempted by academic demands, grades, and changing bells. Teachers may have been able to avoid the real concerns and feelings of their students. This difference in orientation could be due in part to teachers' role perception and their focus towards learning. Can and should learning be fun? The junior high teachers did not seem to recognize themselves as motivators—motivating students was not a deeply felt role.

Center for Early Adolescence Studies

During this same period, researchers at the Center for Early Adolescence in Carrboro, North Carolina, undertook a study of schools which had been identified, according to their criteria, as being particularly responsive to the developmental needs of young adolescents (Dorman, 1983; Lipsitz, 1984). Selecting from among many that were nominated, the researchers identified four schools to be observed in great depth. At the end of the intensive observations, the researchers concluded that, while there was no single model that could be prescribed exclusively, there were common themes present in each of the four highly successful schools. Lipsitz (1984, p. 167) described the most striking of these common features as the schools' "willingness and ability to adapt all school practices to the individual differences in intellectual, biological and social maturation of their students." Educators in these schools set out to establish a positive learning climate, not just because it would lead to increased academic achievement, but because it was something which possessed intrinsic value in the education of young adolescents.

These middle schools were successful because they built their programs on an understanding of and a commitment to the characteristics of early adolescents as learners and human beings. To respond positively to these students, all of the four schools stressed the fact that they were not secondary schools based on a junior or high school model.

Each school used an organizational strategy that helped develop a sense of community in a group small enough for early adolescents to feel real membership; each school produced smallness within bigness. While none of the four schools had the exact same method or organizing students, all had a house or team structure, some of which were organized so that multiage grouping permitted the teachers and students to experience the long term relationships which other researchers have begun to identify as significant. As Lipsitz (1984, 194) expressed it, the team or house:

> ...minimizes size, personalizes the environment,
> increases communication among students and teachers, and reduces tension. The schools have all reduced
> the influence of subject-oriented departments in order
> to empower multidisciplinary teams. They have guaranteed teachers common planning periods so that ev-

ery student is known predictably by a team of teachers who have time to consult with one another about his or her academic progress and general well-being. The common planning period also promotes collegiality and professionalism in curriculum development and review.

Reinforcing the conclusions that Doda reached about the effect of the team organization on teacher perspectives, Lipsitz observed that the "psychic rewards for teaching in these schools are high," and that there is a highly unusual lack of adult isolation in the schools (Lipsitz, p. 186-7):

Common planning and lunch periods, team meetings, and team teaching encourage constant communication and allow for high levels of companionship. Teachers are not abandoned to their students, which is very important in working with the age group, with which daily experiences may not necessarily be rewarding.

In an earlier summary of the research, Lipsitz (n.d., p. 6) concluded:

Finally, while it is not possible to say how widespread excellence in middle-grade schooling is, we can conclude from these four schools that young adolescents and adults can live and learn together in peaceable school communities; that dichotomies like quality vs. equity and academic vs. social goals need not be mutually exclusive; and that with diverse means and in diverse circumstances, middle schools can be breeding grounds for academic excellence and social development.

Another outlier-style examination of the characteristics of effective inner-city intermediate schools (Levine, 1984) contained descriptions of schools in Watts, Brooklyn, the Bronx, and Detroit. These schools, with demonstrably higher academic achievement than others in the same situations, were found to have undergone "significant structural change" on the way to improvement. Organizational arrangements which created a more personal environment, or in Rutter's language, an "ethos of caring," were high on the list of effective innovations. Team organization which facilitated group planning and students' personal growth were at the heart of the improvement process.

Levine (p. 711) and his colleagues concluded:

> We believe that significant structural change is a requirement for effective instruction at inner-city secondary schools; efforts to improve teaching methods at inner-city junior high schools are not likely to have much impact unless accompanied by appropriate structural changes in instructional and organizational arrangements.

Conclusion

The research from the 1980s on the education of young adolescents made it clear that concerns like the name of the school or the grade levels were less important to the outcomes of students than factors related to school organization. Furthermore, this period of research made it clear that another reason much of the research had been fruitless, to that point, was the false assumption that the middle school reorganization process has been, primarily, one of change in the curriculum offered to the students or of new instructional strategies to present the materials to be learned.

In the early 90s, there remained little evidence for the view that changes in curriculum and instruction have been central to the middle school movement. Much of what students learned in the eighth grade was the same regardless of the school in which they learned it. The curriculum and instruction students experienced was probably what their parents also experienced, or endured. While it may be accurate to argue that changes in the curriculum and instructional program of schools for early adolescents should have come first, this has apparently not been the case. Perhaps the attempts to change the curriculum that did occur were short-lived because, as Levine wrote, they were too often implemented without important corresponding changes in the organization of the school.

By the mid-80s research in middle level education suggested that organizational restructuring had occurred in a growing number of schools, and that this reorganization was very similar, even though it occurred in very diverse school settings and in very diverse communities. Furthermore, the research had begun to suggest that these efforts at reorganization did, indeed, promote higher academic achievement and improved personal development for the youth who were among the fortunate few who experienced such a program.

SUMMARY OF RESEARCH ON MIDDLE SCHOOL EDUCATION PRIOR TO 1985

❑ Much of the early research was an illusory and inappropri-
ately global comparison of middle school and junior high
schools which were similar in virtually every way. Hence,
the research found little or no difference between the two
types of schools.

❑ Research did demonstrate an emerging consensus on the
essential components of exemplary middle schools, those
which were believed to successfully address the developmental needs of young adolescents.

❑ Implementation of the middle school concept appeared to be
more successful in the area of school organization during
this period, and less successful in the areas of curriculum and
instruction.

❑ A few schools which accurately incorporated the organizational principles of the middle school concept, similar to
those of the effective schools movement, were able to
demonstrate important outcomes in student achievement,
personal development, and group citizenship.

❑ The number of schools effectively implementing even the
organizational components of the middle school concept was
small, compared to the growing number of schools identified
as middle schools.

RESEARCH ON MIDDLE SCHOOL EDUCATION: 1985-1994

From 1985 to 1994, research on middle school education proceeded at a rapid pace. Since 1988, for example, 2,141 citations relating to middle school education have appeared in ERIC, the clearinghouse for educational research; of these citations, 1,245 included references to research in some area of middle school education. A total of 594 of these studies focused on some aspect of achievement, with 379 touching directly on the topic of academic achievement in middle schools. In the area of doctoral dissertation research (a vast, virtually untapped well of knowledge), hundreds of studies had researched various aspects of middle level education. Major studies with a national scope had been undertaken by research groups, and private foundations funded and published many similar efforts. Of all of this vigorous effort, the research which is relevant to this monograph focused largely on three different, but related areas.

One dominant theme in the literature of middle level education during the last decade has been aimed at documenting what appeared to be a relatively final national consensus on the desirable characteristics of middle level schools. In one year alone, three major organizations (Cawelti, 1989; Alexander and McEwin, 1989; Carnegie Council, 1989) published their lists of essential middle school components, with a striking congruence among the desired features. Departments of education in state after state (e.g., California: Superintendent's Middle Grade Task Force, 1987) have issued similar pronouncements for middle schools in their own dominions. Interdisciplinary team organization, advisory programs, flexible scheduling and grouping, enriched curriculum experiences, broadened opportunities for student recognition and success, more active instruction and learning, articulation to schools above and below, shared decision-making, parent and community involvement—all are now a part of a solid national consensus about the most central features of effective schools for early adolescents in the remaining years of this century. Achieving this consensus has been neither easily or quickly done, and it is, we think, reason for some celebration.

> **A solid national consensus about the most central features of effective schools for early adolescents has emerged.**

A second central theme of research on middle school education in the last decade, closely aligned with the first, has been the continued attempt to determine the degree to which these desirable features of exemplary middle level education had been implemented in the daily experiences of the nation's middle school students. Here, it seems most reasonable to say, more than modest celebration would be premature. There is, however, an increasing amount of evidence to suggest that educators have made what must be regarded as a great deal of progress in implementing the middle school concept in an increasingly greater number of school sites and situations.

The Alexander and McEwin study (1989), commissioned by the National Middle School Association, included the benefit of a review of progress from an earlier benchmark study (Alexander, 1968). These scholars were able to document what can safely be described as a substantial increase, during the intervening 20 years, in the implementation of basic middle school components in schools across the country. They reported, for example, an increase in schools utilizing an interdisciplinary organization of teachers and students, from 3% in 1968 to approximately 35% in 1988. Advisory programs were not even developed to the point where they could be usefully included in the 1968 survey, but by 1988, 39% of the schools reported an advisory program.

A survey of national practices and trends conducted at almost the same time by Epstein and Mac Iver (1990) affirmed the findings of the Alexander and McEwin (1989) effort. Among the schools surveyed in this study, even though 25% reported having nothing resembling a teacher-based classroom advisory program, 28% reported having a strong advisory program. Close to 40% of the schools reported being organized into interdisciplinary teams rather than self-contained class-rooms or high school-style academic departments. Fully functioning teams, with common planning time focused on teamwork of various kinds were, however, far less often encountered; approximately 10% of schools reported such operations. Epstein and Mac Iver went so far as to assert that instruction, in the average middle school, was likely to be more innovative, active, and student-centered than in other grade organizations serving the same students (p. 34).

Increasingly, doctoral dissertation research confirmed the greater implementation of essential middle school concepts, such as the above, in more and more schools. Venerable (1993), for example, demon-strated the considerable progress which had taken place in the state of Arizona, not generally known as one of the pioneers in implementing middle school programs. Ritzenthaler (1993) drew the same conclu-sions about middle level schools in the state of Florida. These results are frequently confirmed by larger studies.

Many state, regional, and district groups have surveyed schools to determine the extent to which recommended programs had been imple-mented. Such reports are generally supportive of the dramatic increases over the last two decades reported by Alexander and McEwin, and by dissertation research. One survey, for example, conducted in 1993, by a regional supervisory association (Bedford, 1993) examined the con-dition of middle school implementation in all of the middle level schools on Long Island, New York. The data indicated that advisory programs were present in about one-third of the schools, a majority of the responding schools featured interdisciplinary team organization, many with common planning time for the teachers involved. Block scheduling, heterogeneous grouping, and interdisciplinary instruction were present in many more schools than would have been the case a decade ago. Similar results are proclaimed by state middle grade policy initiatives such as those reported by Georgia (Georgia Board of Education, 1993).

When researchers attempted to shape the sample of schools involved in such a survey toward those supposed to be exemplary pro grams, the results, as would be expected, were even more positive. In the first edition of the current report (George & Oldaker, 1985), for example, the sample of schools was drawn in a way intended to represent exemplary schools. Schools in this study had been recognized for their exemplary status locally, nationally, and in some cases, internationally. Asked to indicate the extent to which they implemented the basic components of the middle school concept, responses were dramatically affirmative. Interdisciplinary teaming was a "central feature" in 90% of the schools. In other areas, 94% reported a flexibly scheduled school day, 93% included a homebase advisory program. Another study of exemplary middle schools (Connors & Gill, 1991) found that school cited as a part of federal recognition programs had implemented significantly more of the components recognized as central to exemplary middle schools.

Some careful studies of daily experiences in middle grades schools have nonetheless, been less than uniformly positive in their descriptions of the presence of basic middle school concepts. Two nationally-conducted shadow studies of life in the sixth (Lounsbury & Johnston, 1988) and eighth (Lounsbury & Clark, 1990) grades, for example, indicated that while reorganization at the school level may have proceeded at remarkable rates over the last decade, life inside the classrooms for sixth and eighth graders has remained relatively stable, and uninspiring.

Lounsbury and Clark concluded that the typical situation in the eighth grade reflected a continuing conflict between prevailing practices and the known needs of early adolescent students. Departmental organization of teachers, students, and the curriculum dominated the lives of most. Schedules remained rigid. Students remained in rigid ability-grouped situations. Passive learning experiences continued, focused on coverage of curriculum content packaged much as the Committee of Ten suggested a century ago. Most studies of the current status of the implementation of middle school principles seemed to agree, at least to a certain point, with these descriptive statements of the situation in general. Epstein and Mac Iver (1990), for example, stated that few schools were organized into houses or other smaller, school-within-school arrangements, cooperative learning was honored more in intention rather than practice, and exploratory, mini-course curriculum enrichment was largely absent.

It is likely, we regret, that in 1994 there are many hundreds, perhaps thousands of middle level schools in America where the awakening call to reform and transformation has not yet been recognized. In these schools, students continue to be expected to learn in organizational arrangements much more appropriate for university graduate students, to struggle by themselves through the thickets of schooling and early adolescence, to motivate themselves to study a curriculum of little utility and less natural interest, in instructional circumstances that Rip Van Winkle would recognize.

In the late 80s, however, a number of reform initiatives were undertaken in response to the exhortations of the national government, and with the special support of agencies like the Carnegie Corporation of New York. Recent reports of these efforts are, on the whole, quite encouraging. In 1992, for example, the Council of Chief State School Officers (Council, 1992) released a report of reforms connected with their Middle School State Policy Initiative. Attempts at middle school improvement in 27 states were described by the Council as "a success story in progress" (p.vii). Early in 1993, the Edna McConnell Clark Foundation (Lewis, 1993) released a similar report of "middle school reform in progress." In a project involving 12 middle schools in five cities, in some of the most challenging settings in American education, the Foundation reported "small miracles that yield significant results. Slowly middle school reform is becoming a reality" (p.12).

How, then, can the current status of the implementation of middle school concepts be characterized? Our judgement is that, considering the deteriorating conditions in school districts and communities around the nation during the last decade, and in spite of the great natural inertia which holds most organizations and many middle level schools in place, progress in the implementation of these concepts has been comparatively swift. Especially when considering the likelihood that "conditions with which the young students in the...schools must cope grew worse during the time that the schools were trying to make better schools for them" (Lewis, 1993). During the past decade the economy went into deep recession, a war was fought in the Middle East, most state education budgets were cut back sharply, and several presidential administrations did little to support local reform efforts other than to chastise those in the schools for their supposed culpability; middle school reform has proceeded in largely unheralded but steady fashion. Middle school reform efforts continued unabated.

> **There are now hundreds of middle schools, some in virtually every state, which offer students a daily educational experience that can be safely described as exemplary.**

It is likely, we think, that there are now hundreds of middle schools, some in virtually every state, which offer students a daily educational experience that can be safely described as exemplary, incorporating virtually all of the elements deemed desireable. In such schools, a vision of the most appropriate education has been built on a compassionate understanding of the nature and needs of young adolescents. These schools are organized into effective interdisciplinary teams, they provide close personal relationships between advisory teachers and students. In these schools, an enriched curriculum is offered to every student, through instructional strategies that are developmentally appropriate. In these same schools, teachers, administrators, and parents regularly meet together to establish the policies, solve the problems, and make the decisions that will carry these schools through a new decade of sustained quality and school improvement.

It is also likely, we argue, that there are now thousands of middle schools, many in every state, where middle level educators have effectively initiated a process of transforming the school which will continue toward successful completion. When completed, this transformation will yield a whole new cadre of exemplary middle schools for the education of the generation which will enter the next century while in the middle grades. Much hope and promise can correctly be attached, we believe, to these emerging middle schools.

The third focus of middle school research in the last decade has been, albeit still prematurely, to accurately decipher the effects of the components of an exemplary middle school, when present, on the achievement, personal development, and attitudes of early adolescent learners. Considering the status of middle school implementation, it is likely that much of this research continued to make specious comparisons of school programs that were more alike than different, and therefore continued to produce results which were either nonexistent or confusing. Even so, we think that promising findings, while yet sparse, have begun to spring up like the tips of crocuses through the snows of early spring.

Most educators, parents, and community members, considering the reorganization to middle school, seem to want to know, first, whether such a move will produce increased academic achievement as measured by standardized tests. At the very least, they want to be assured that middle school will not threaten achievement, while producing benefits in other areas like more positive student personal development or aspects of improved group citizenship. It is and always has been, of course, quite difficult, if not impossible, to produce school-based data which can be identified as correlates of substantially increased achievement.

Several decades of research on school and teacher effectiveness, to which we referred above, made it clear that socioeconomic status is not the only determinent of academic achievement. But factors other than the "home effect," are not simple or easy to detect or demonstrate, and it may be impossible to demonstrate school effects which are greater than the home effect. Recently, Paul Barton, of the Educational Testing Service was said (Will, 1993) to have estimated that about 90 percent of the differences in academic achievement within and between schools can be attributed to five factors that have much more to do with home than school. According to Barton, those five factors include the following:

1. number of days absent from school.
2. number of hours spent watching television.
3. number of pages read for homework.
4. quantity and quality of reading material in the home.
5. the presence of two parents in the home.

Considering the difficulty of demonstrating direct correlations between school programs, including the components of the middle school, and substantial differences in academic achievement, it is not surprising that research on middle school components, undertaken in the last decade, had difficulty making this connection clearly and convincingly (Clay, 1992; Dirks, 1992; Ernest, 1991; Lawrence, 1989; McGrath, 1991; McPartland, 1991; Pinegar, 1990; Worley, 1992). This is particularly less than surprising when considering that middle school is a "work in progress." Research efforts in middle school education, which failed to first ensure that an exemplary middle school program was in place, were doomed it seems, to produce less than affirmative outcomes. Demands for the demonstration of guaranteed increases in academic achievement made of a movement which is far from having reached any sense of completion are worse than premature; they are impossible to satisfy. It may be that those who insist on making such demands are aware of the impossibility of what they ask; if not, they need to be told. In spite of all of these disclaimers, however, by 1994, some evidence did exist which suggested that when all of the elements of an exemplary middle school are in place and functioning as they were intended, positive outcomes can be expected.

> **...as each year passes, more and more studies are able to demonstrate significant effects in the area of academic achievement which favor the middle school concept.**

In our judgement, one of the most important trends in research in middle school education is that as each year passes, more and more studies are able to demonstrate significant effects in the area of academic achievement which favor the middle school concept.

Some of this evidence comes from large scale statistical studies. Lee and Smith (1993) used data from the National Longitudinal Study of 1988, involving 8,845 eighth grade students from 377 middle level schools nationwide. They were able to document that middle school concepts had a positive, albeit modest, effect on students' achievement and engagement in their studies. De-emphasizing departmentalization in favor of more interdisciplinary organization, more heterogeneous grouping, and increased team teaching also contributed to the more equitable distribution of achievement and engagement among students of different social backgrounds.

Some of that evidence has come from the results at foundation-sponsored reform efforts, often in the most challenging situations. The Clark Foundation's attempts to improve the educational experience of inner city youngsters by implementing middle school concepts, while less successful than they would have liked, resulted in having student achievement improve in half of the schools in the project, and "students indicated in many ways other than test scores that they were being encouraged by the school changes around them" (Lewis, 1993, p. 26). What may be more important for achievement in the long term, the foundation reported that "In almost every school, teachers will tell you that they have come to truly believe that their students can learn at a high level and that they have gained new skills to teach them." (p. 24). Encouraging situations like this suggest that the next decade may witness even more positive outcomes, especially considering the recent systematic efforts undertaken by this and other foundations such as the Kellogg Foundation, the Lilly Endowment, the Carnegie Corporation, and even large corporations like Champion who have recognized and supported the promise of the middle school movement.

A few other studies have begun to yield academic achievement results which favor the middle school concept. Data from the Maine Educational Assessment in 1991, for example, indicated (Norton, 1991) that students who had received their middle level education where the components of the concept were in place consistently outscored other students by a wide margin, in every area tested by the statewide assessment: reading, mathematics, writing, science, social studies, and humanities.

Dissertation research conducted during the last 5-8 years has begun to indicate an even more positive pattern in academic achievement, as well as factors relating to student personal development. Myers (1988), for example, was able to demonstrate that eighth graders in middle schools "which are strong in implementing middle school principles had higher achievement than eighth graders who attend other middle and junior high schools." Doran (1989), Bryan (1987), Ferrara (1993), Hall (1993), Warren (1993), and Barris (1993) all drew similar conclusions in their studies. In each of these studies, when components of the middle school were determined to be effectively in place, academic achievement benefited.

> **When components of the middle school were determined to be effectively in place, academic achievement benefited.**

Two factors may explain this promising new trend. First, more and more middle schools are implementing the concepts which distinguish them from more traditional middle level schools, so that research is actually beginning to measure programs and organizational arrangements that are, in fact, different; a situation very unlike the early studies making comparisons between the middle school and junior high programs. Second, researchers have begun to design their work so that actual program components (e.g., interdisciplinary team organization) are the focus of their studies, rather than global comparisons of schools where the primary differences may be in the name or the grade levels in the schools. ❏

SUMMARY OF RESEARCH ON MIDDLE SCHOOL EDUCATION, 1985-94

❑ A national consensus on the characteristics of the exemplary middle school has been reached.

❑ Substantial national progress has been made in the successful implementation of the components comprising the exemplary middle school.

❑ When compared to schools where such programs are absent, schools effectively implementing the characteristics of the exemplary middle school are increasingly able to demonstrate positive outcomes related to academic achievement and student personal development.

Part Two

EFFECTIVENESS OF MIDDLE LEVEL SCHOOLS

THE 1985 SURVEY

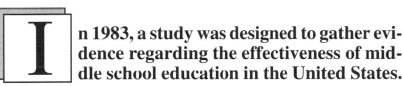

I **n 1983, a study was designed to gather evidence regarding the effectiveness of middle school education in the United States.**
In particular, two areas were investigated:

1. the extent to which middle schools identified as exemplary contained program components which conformed to the recommendations of the literature on middle school education; and

2. the outcomes of such programs.

Central office staff members and school administrators in 34 states, involving 160 schools, were invited to supply evidence about the existence of certain programs and of the positive and negative effects of the implementation of middle school programs in their districts.

A list of reputedly exemplary middle schools was developed from middle schools identified by: (1) the 1982 Study of Well-disciplined Schools sponsored by Phi Delta Kappa; (2) the 1983 U.S.D.O.E. National Secondary School Recognition Program; (3) a panel of ten persons recognized as experts in middle school education; and (4) several lists of exemplary schools identified in recent books on middle school education. Of this number, 130 schools responded, yielding a return rate of 81%.

Limitations and Assumptions

The findings of the first study applied most directly to middle schools which contained the components referred to in the description of the sample which follows. No attempt was made to control or to analyze data on the basis of socioeconomic status, school size, geographic location, or the influence of school leadership or talented instruction.

The study was also limited by the fact that respondents were encouraged to supply evidence regarding the positive effects of middle school education in their districts. Negative data, while sought, were not as strenuously pursued. It is possible, therefore, that as a consequence of the design of the study, the few persons who failed to respond may have done so because they had fewer positive experiences to relate, and that those who did respond may have elected to exclude negative data.

REPRESENTATIONS OF THE EXEMPLARY MIDDLE SCHOOL

Responding schools reported, in 1985, substantially greater incorporation of the middle school concept than recorded shortly thereafter by Cawelti (1989), Alexander & McEwin (1989), or Epstein & MacIver (1990). Interdisciplinary team organization was a central feature of 90% of the schools in the study. Common groups of students taught by an interdisciplinary team of teachers who are located closely together and who have common planning periods was the rule in the schools in this study. While an even larger percentage of schools (94%) provided for a flexibly scheduled school day that permitted teams of teachers to modify their programs as they believed wise, 93% included a home-base, advisor-advisee program for each child. In the 1985 study, 99% of the respondents reported a continuing effort to focus the curriculum on student personal development as well as academic achievement. One hundred percent of the respondents indicated that administrators and teachers collaborated in making the decisions that shaped school-wide policies affecting students. Clearly, these data indicated that the schools in that national sample had achieved far greater than typical inclusion of the central organizational components of the middle school philosophy. They were alike organizationally, and that likeness reflected a commitment to the implementation of concepts at the heart of the middle school movement.

This was not, of course, a random sample of middle level schools. It was, in fact, an attempt to draw responses from an atypical group of schools, ones that had been recognized for excellence in educating the early adolescent student. The purpose of the study was to ascertain the degree to which these exemplary schools incorporated the components of the middle school concept and the outcomes which could be associated with such schools.

Student Achievement

The findings of the 1985 study disputed earlier opinions that academic achievement is either unaffected or only modestly improved by a move to middle school organization. Rather than the typical finding of no differences, sixty-two percent of the respondents in this study described consistent academic improvement. An additional twenty-eight percent of the respondents supplied specific results demonstrating increased scores on state assessment tests, the California Achievement Test, the Iowa Test of Basic Skills, and similar tests since their schools became middle schools. An overwhelming majority, eighty-five percent, observed that teacher confidence in student abilities had increased, which, many suggested, led to higher expectations and greater student productivity in academic classes. Other aspects of reorganized programs positively affecting student learning included coordination of skills and subjects by interdisciplinary teams as well as greater teacher awareness of preadolescent needs and abilities.

School Discipline

Incorporating the middle school concept improved school discipline in almost every measurable manner in these schools. Tardiness and truancy moderately or greatly decreased, according to a majority of respondents, as did school vandalism and theft. Approximately 80% noted a significant reduction in office referrals and suspensions, while close to 60% expelled fewer students after the transition. Almost 90% observed that teacher and staff confidence in managing disruptive students increased, diminishing administrative involvement in discipline in many schools. Reorganization to an exemplary middle school program clearly improved school and classroom discipline.

> **Reorganization to an exemplary middle school program clearly improved school and classroom discipline.**

Student Personal Development

The 1985 study indicated that exemplary middle schools had been very successful in promoting student personal development. Student emotional health, creativity, and confidence in self-directed learning were positively affected by reorganization, testified over 80% of the respondents; better than 90% believed that student self-concept and social development benefited, too. Anecdotal evidence overwhelmingly credited middle school programs with enhancing each student's personal and social skills. The success of team organization and teacher-based guidance in helping individuals develop closer peer relationships was cited repeatedly. Extracurricular and intramural athletic activities were designed to provide opportunities for all students instead of a precious few and invited greater student participation, interaction, and competition. Awards for leadership, good citizenship, and cooperation in and out of classes enabled those who weren't honor roll students or star athletes to experience the important satisfaction of recognition before peers. Interdisciplinary teams, classroom guidance, and exploratory programs increased opportunities for student involvement and accomplishments, significantly improving student personal development, according to respondents. Reorganization was also identified as a chance to delay certain social pressures that seemed to precipitate an undesirable sophistication in young people. Schools could work with students before major growth spurts associated with puberty occurred and could help them adjust to new academic environments before problems developed.

School Learning Climate

In the 1980s, studies analyzing school effectiveness had correlated the atmosphere or learning climate with student behavior and achievement. Students who felt valued by teachers and who viewed school as more than just a place to meet friends tended to show respect for their schools in many ways. The exemplary middle schools in the 1985 study developed programs that demonstrated persistent caring for students as young people and created a school environment to meet their special academic and personal needs. Predictably, respondents supplied evidence indicating stronger school spirit since reorganization. Over ninety-five percent of them declared that student attitudes toward school and feelings about teachers were moderately or strongly positive, as a consequence of reorganization. Eighty-six percent witnessed greater student participation in special interest activities, while seventy-five percent noted better attendance at their middle schools. Anecdotal descriptions of student enthusiasm for an involvement in school programs ran nearly five to one in favor of changes brought about by a move to middle school organization.

— 45 —

In discussions of school district reorganization from junior high to middle schools, concern or fear that changing programs will diminish school spirit had often been expressed. Educators and citizens argued heatedly about the proper role of interscholastic competition and accompanying functions like cheer leading and athletic awards. Proponents of such activities predicted that eliminating them will negatively affect school spirit; opponents stressed that their inclusion in schools meant most students would be excluded from participating and recognition, weakening school spirit. The 1985 survey indicated that when middle school curriculum was designed to encourage greater student involvement in different ways, removal or significant modification of interscholastic sports programs did not diminish student pride and positive feelings. Failure to compensate for altering conventional athletic competition during reorganization, however, may have been costly to school pride.

The majority of respondents identified new activities that effectively replaced traditional ones in generating student excitement and participation. Advisory group and interdisciplinary team programs successfully stimulated students to get involved in their schools, as did offering intramural, clubs, exploratory classes, and awards for effort and excellence. Several schools retained interscholastic sports and cheer leading by restructuring them to include more students or by shifting responsibility for them to community agencies allowed to use school facilities after hours.

Faculty Morale

In 1985, an impressive ninety-four percent of the respondents described staff morale and rapport as moderately or strongly positive following reorganization. Based on formal and informal observations, ninety-three percent concluded that a move to middle school organization favorably influenced staff attitude toward change, and eighty-two percent noticed increased staff participation in special interest activities following the transition. Over one-half of the respondents cited lower teacher absenteeism and turnover as indications of high morale, noting teachers fought transfers to other schools. All anecdotal comments but one praised the benefits to morale of implementing middle school philosophy. Teachers voiced greater job satisfaction, worked more closely, and spent more leisure time together, said respondents.

Such positive faculty morale had not magically appeared when the middle schools opened their doors. Some faculty members lacked enthusiasm for reorganization, refusing to cooperate with efforts to involve them in the planning process. A noticeable number of secondary-trained teachers thought the new expectations of them were unreasonable and resisted change. As they enjoyed increased support on teams and more control over learning time, however, many skeptical teachers developed an appreciation for the appropriateness of middle school programs. Even those disillusioned with district policies and budgets, by a national clamor for educational reform, or with contract negotiations, often admitted later that reorganization improved schooling and made their jobs more rewarding. One respondent's comment that it took ten years before his staff truly supported the middle school concept suggests that considerable patience may be a prerequisite for developing strong faculty morale. Other comments expressed concern about the life span of staff enthusiasm in middle schools, mentioning that some teachers could over-extend themselves and tire within a few years if precautions were not taken.

> 66 **Previously isolated instructors became team members and developed the same sense of belonging and camaraderie they hoped to instill in their students.**

One particular middle school program component believed by respondents to contribute greatly to staff morale was the interdisciplinary team organization. Previously isolated instructors became team members and developed the same sense of belonging and camaraderie they hoped to instill in their students. The flexibility in scheduling inherent to team responsibility for a common group of students occupying generally the same area provided teachers with many options for instruction. Sharing knowledge of students and subjects increased their confidence and consistency.

Staff Development

Reorganization to middle schools, according to respondents in the 1985 study, provided ample opportunities for teachers, principals, and district administrators to coordinate efforts to improve instruction and classroom management by implementing extensive staff development programs. Acknowledging that some teachers were more responsive to change than others and that occasionally staff members had been worn down by too much inservice training, the exemplary middle school administrators in this survey nonetheless noted greater staff involvement in designing and executing philosophy, curriculum, and objectives when they conducted staff development programs to facilitate reorganization. Inservice programs about characteristics of the age group, interdisciplinary teaming, and advisory/advisee groups, supplemented with educational programs applicable to all grades, such as Effective Schooling, Instruction Theory Into Practice, Assertive Discipline, and Reality Therapy, brought to the middle school staff research findings and practices that can revitalize teaching and learning in these crucial grades. Most schools assessed needs and interests of their teachers prior to, during, and after the transition, enlisted the aid of local universities and colleges when possible, encouraged individual and group attendance at state and national conferences about middle school education, and generally scheduled dozens of inservice sessions to improve instruction.

Teacher receptivity to staff development, characterized by greater participation in inservice education and favorable responses to surveys undertaken at different times during reorganization, was and continued to be positive, particularly when teachers were involved in the planning of the transition from the beginning. Respondents considered such teacher involvement crucial to establishing successful middle schools and indicated that teachers in the middle truly appreciated a concerted effort to develop an educational program specifically tailored to accommodate their students. Frequently, well-established middle school programs produced faculty members who served willingly as resources for newly reorganized schools; teachers and administrators became consultants for other districts. If done well, moving to middle schools was an excellent opportunity to implement effective staff development that involved and excited teachers who too often felt ignored and beleaguered.

> **" Teacher involvement is crucial to establishing successful middle schools.**

Parental Involvement and Support

Respondents to the 1985 survey proudly described the positive parental involvement and support they experienced after reorganization to middle schools. They cited better attendance at open houses, conferences, and PTA meetings as well as a greater propensity to volunteer as chaperones for field trips, dances, or other school socials. Parents offered to help in libraries, cafeterias, and classrooms, to coach intramural athletics, and to teach mini courses in many of the exemplary middle schools. Administrators in these schools cultivated parental involvement during all stages of the transition, anticipating the contributions and support that parents could give to the new program. They took pains to explain why and how reorganization would improve schooling for their children and established communication channels that encouraged parents to ask questions and to make suggestions at any point of the move to the middle school.

Observing that most parents welcomed invitations to become involved in their children's schools, they sought to capitalize on parental willingness to share responsibility for their children's education and were well-rewarded for their efforts. One respondent boasted that parents told him, "You cannot change your program until my last child has gone through it!" Another said, "My child likes school for the first time." Others noted that parents of their students rallied to prevent tampering with successful programs, such as team organization and small group advisory periods. Parents often voiced support for the middle school at board meetings and frequently voted to fund the money needed to maintain the level of educational services characteristics of exemplary middle schools. Like the majority of middle school teachers, middle school parents genuinely appreciated the attention focused on their children's learning and behavioral needs by conscientious reorganization and were eager to help middle schools meet these needs.

Community Involvement and Support/Media Coverage

Admitting that community concern for the cost of public education could spell financial trouble for school programs, particularly for reorganizational plans needing money to provide facilities and to retrain staff, in 1985, respondents nonetheless reported favorable community support. Businesses, civic organizations, and community leaders resembled the parents in their willingness to contribute to the schooling of middle level students when invited to do so by administrators and teachers in exemplary middle schools. They both attended and presented assemblies, fund-raising events, and career awareness programs, generating and diffusing valuable support for the middle school throughout the community. People with and without children in the schools volunteered to cover classes, to tutor exceptional students, and to sponsor clubs, according to many administrators in our survey. "All we have to do is ask!" wrote one respondent of his community's eagerness to help in the school. Others related that although they would like to have even more community involvement and support, they were generally pleased with existing levels. Those who brought different elements of the community, such as a policemen, alcohol and drug abuse counselors, and public relations experts from businesses and corporations, into their schools as resources for the curriculum to promote civic awareness and responsibility noted definite improvements in student behavior and attitudes. The schools and surrounding communities benefited from such combined efforts to present a balanced program for students in middle grades. Support became mutual, sincere, and effective when nurtured during reorganization and carefully sustained afterwards.

Three-fourths of the respondents reported that newspaper, radio, and television coverage was positive during the reorganization, although a few wished it had been more in-depth and consistent. Districts employing professional public relations officers to convey school news to the media noticed greatly improved coverage; others were pleased that certain middle school components differing from traditional junior high programs, such as team organization and advisory efforts, caught reporters' eyes and were publicized, giving exemplary middle schools occasion to explain and to justify these differences. Many of the exemplary middle schools surveyed had received national recognition for excellence and enjoyed particularly favorable press, sometimes to the chagrin of other schools in the district or region. Most respondents hoped to improve media coverage of their programs by continuing to develop successful learning environments appropriate for their students.

One-fourth of the respondents lamented the lack of favorable press their school received during reorganization, stating that the media in their areas publicized conflicts between the school board and superintendent or shortcomings of the educational system more zealously than they praised instructional programs. Their comments suggested that sensationalism and criticism of local schools appeared to be more newsworthy and that having positive reports printed or telecast was difficult.

> **In stark contrast to the strong vote of confidence given to reorganization by middle school parents, teachers, and surrounding communities in 1985, support wavered among high school staff.**

High School Staff Perceptions

In stark contrast to the strong vote of confidence given to reorganization by middle school parents, teachers, and surrounding communities, in 1985, support wavered among high school staff. Just over half of exemplary middle schools surveyed reported praise and approval from the upper grade teachers to whom they sent students. Most of these added that to earn such good marks, they had to overcome earlier suspicions and fears voiced by high school teachers doubting the seriousness of middle school programs. Many acknowledged district emphasis on K-12 curriculum and articulation as very helpful in establishing positive reputations and relations with high schools. A few noted that reorganization inspired some high school teachers to improve their programs by implementing ninth grade interdisciplinary teams and by maintaining the close parent-teacher-student contact developed in the middle grades. Respondents indicated great pride when told by senior high staff that the middle school years must be doing something right since students were well-prepared for their final school years. Even this group enjoying favorable opinion from their secondary counterparts, however, expressed difficulty in pleasing high school personnel.

The other forty-six percent of the respondents reported criticism, fickle support, or apathy toward their programs. Often high school teachers said that middle schools were too elementary, that only they in the upper grades really teach, and that it would be a step down to teach in middle school. The absence of ability grouping and interscholastic athletics was thought to disrupt high school programs, eliciting more negative comments. If reorganization moved ninth graders to high schools, contributed to overcrowding, or required a greater budget than allotted to the high school, many instructors there were quick to disregard any merit assessed by a program based on preadolescent needs. Dissatisfaction in high school perceptions of middle schools was apparent, but many respondents suggested that schools at all levels should work hard to improve communication and cooperation. A few proposed re-assigning district teachers to different buildings and grades more often and encouraging K- 12 articulation to promote positive feelings among schools.

SUMMARY AND CONCLUSIONS: THE 1985 SURVEY

❏ Middle schools identified as exemplary, in 1985, implemented a substantial degree of the programs deemed
desirable for the education of young adolescents.

❏ Middle schools identified as exemplary, in 1985, reported substantially positive outcomes associated with
the implementation of program components thought to
be desirable for the education of young adolescents.

❏ The data from the 1985 survey foreshadowed the emerging research support for the middle school concept
which would come during the next decade.

Results indicated that, in 1985, middle schools which had a reputation as highly successful were very similar in terms of the components of the program. The programs common to these exemplary middle schools did tend to conform to the recommendations in the literature of middle level education then, and in 1994. Furthermore, when implemented in this way, the results appeared to be dramatically positive. Academic achievement, student behavior, school learning climate, faculty morale, staff development, and a number of other factors were affected in positive ways.

The results of this study did not, of course, indicate that other programs for the organization and operation of middle level schools were necessarily less effective. The 1985 study also did not indicate whether the results enjoyed by the schools in this study were or were not present in other middle schools which have not been designated as exemplary. A study of a similar sample of more conventional junior high schools identified as highly successful, or a sample of other middle schools which have not been so identified, might not, it was noted, yield similar results. Other explanations, (e.g., a Hawthorne effect) might have been responsible for the reported outcomes of the reorganization; or it may have simply reflected a change to a less turbulent period in American education. The study needed to be replicated, at a later time with a broader sample but ones which still represented schools which had undertaken rigorous attempts to implement the middle school concept. ❏

Part
Three

THE EFFECTIVE
MIDDLE SCHOOL

THE 1993 SURVEY

I n the spring of 1993, a survey was designed
to update the evidence available regarding the presence and effectiveness of
middle school components in schools for young adolescents. The 1993 survey was parallel, in several ways, to the survey originally reported in 1985 and summarized in Part Two. It was
intended to re-examine the extent to which the middle school concept
had been implemented in the middle schools in the survey. The survey
also attempted to ascertain the outcomes associated with the implementation of these programs. The 1993 survey, however, was different
from its predecessor in two ways.

First, the sample for the 1993 survey was drawn from a group of
300 schools, representing virtually every state, which had been recommended by a panel of professors of middle school education or by rep-
resentatives of the state department of education where the school
was located. No attempt was made to determine the degree to which
these schools were exemplary, beyond their nomination by professionals in the field. The sample was, by intention, *not* a random sample of
middle level schools from around the nation. We believe that the respondents to the 1993 survey represent a group of schools where serious but not necessarily completely successful attempts have been made

to implement middle school concepts in an exemplary way. These schools represent, we hope, mainstream "middle school," perhaps more than either lighthouse exemplary schools or the typical schools found in a purely random sample of American middle level schools.

Second, the survey attempted to distinguish among schools which had been middle schools for less than five years and those which had been middle schools for more than five years. We hoped that we could learn something important about the experience of educators in schools that were relatively new compared to those which had maintained a middle school program for some greater period of time. Approximately 1/3 (37%) of the respondents were from schools where middle school programs had been in existence for less than five years. Approximately 2/3 (63%) of the schools had been middle schools for more than five years. Among those described as "new" middle schools, the average school was three years old. Those characterized as "old" middle schools had been middle schools for an average of 14 years. The median number of years a responding school had been organized as a middle school was ten.

Limitations and Assumptions

The findings of the 1993 survey apply most directly to schools which have seriously attempted to implement the components of the exemplary middle school. No attempt was made to control or to analyze data on the basis of socioeconomic status of students, school size, geographic locations, or the influence of school leadership. No quantitative manipulations of the data have been attempted, other than conversion to percentages. Selection and interpretations of respondents comments, summaries, and conclusions can be characterized as descriptive and impressionistic.

The study is further limited in that respondents were encouraged to supply evidence regarding the positive effects of middle school concepts in their schools. Negative data, while invited, may not have been perceived by respondents as equally desired by the researchers. Finally, the findings of the study are limited by the return rate of 36%. Of the 300 schools receiving surveys, 108 returned usable responses. The researchers believed that this rate was due to the lengthy (12 pages) and complex nature of the survey and to the fact that no follow-up mailings or phone calls were made to increase the size of the return.

RESULTS OF THE 1993 STUDY

Respondents in both "new" and "old" middle schools were asked to indicate the extent to which components of the middle school concept were in place in their schools. Table One identifies the components and the percentage of responding schools, averaging ten years in operation as middle schools, indicating that the component was *mod cratcly to well developed* in their school. When a school reported a component to be totally absent, that number is represented in parentheses. The remaining schools reported that the component was "minimally developed." For example, 23% of the schools reported that a teacher-based advisory program was at least (or, only) minimally developed.

The data in Table One reveal several interesting features about the schools responding to the 1993 survey. First, they reported that they have implemented the components of the middle school concept more thoroughly than the schools represented in earlier national surveys of random samples of middle level schools (Alexander & McEwin, 1989; Epstein & Mac Iver, 1989). This, we think, was because the schools in the present survey were not randomly selected, having previously been identified as either exemplary or having vigorously attempted to implement the components of the middle school concept. By definition, then, these schools would have been more likely to have gone further in the implementation process. This logic is supported by the fact that the reporting schools described themselves as slightly less fully developed than the schools from the 1985 survey. This may have been, we think, because of the sample of schools used in the 1993 survey. The differences between the two surveys may also have reflected the passage of years and/or the challenges associated with maintaining exemplary programs for a decade or more. The schools in both the 1985 and the 1993 surveys do, nonetheless, report the incorporation of fundamental middle school concepts at a level beyond what has been reported in

Table 1: Percentage of Schools Indicating Degree of Implementation of Middle School Components

Component	Percent Moderate to Well-developed	Percent Absent
Teacher-based advisory program	66	21
Flexible (perhaps block) schedule	75	6
Interdisciplinary team organization	87	3
Organizational arrangements that permit long-term teacher-student relationships (e.g., school-within-a-school; student-teacher progression; multiage grouping)	54	20
Interdisciplinary thematic curriculum	71	
Regular use of alternative instructional strategies	80	
Wide range of exploratory opportunities	82	2
A regular, systematic, authentic, shared decision-making process	91	1
Flexible grouping strategies, primarily heterogeneous	97	1
Transition to high school where teaming and/or advisory are utilized	40	33

other surveys; they are, if self-reports are to be accepted, practicing the middle school philosophy organizationally and programmatically.

Respondents from virtually all schools, in both surveys (covering a period of approximately a decade) indicated strong commitments to several program components, in particular. Between 90-100% indicate an organizational structure featuring interdisciplinary team organization, with a correspondingly flexible schedule, and a matching flexible, primarily heterogeneous process in grouping students for instruction. The same high degree of commitment can be found for the shared decision-making process, where adults in the building work together to solve the problems, establish the policies, and make the decisions that guide the school on a daily, monthly, and yearly basis.

Two components of the concept were described as less fully developed in responding schools. These two components have, until recently, been exceptionally uncommon elements of middle school education: long-term teacher-student relationships; and, close programmatic relationships with neighboring high schools. The fact that 54% of respondents reported that long-term relationships were a part of their organizational scheme (e.g., a school-within-school arrangement) is, upon reflection, an extremely high figure. And, thinking about the frequently ruptured connections between middle and high school programs, 40% is a very substantial proportion of middle schools now feeding into high schools with academic teaming or advisory programs. There may be several explanations for these reports, and future research is urgently needed to clarify these representations.

Schools identified as "new" were asked to complete a 40-item inventory of identifiable effects of reorganization implementing the middle school concept. Respondents were asked to indicate if an effect was noted, and whether those effects when noted, were positive or negative. In virtually every case, respondents replied that notable effects of the transition to middle school had been predominantly positive. That is, in both Tables 2 and 3 below where positive outcomes are reported, the percentage of positive responses is *not* matched by a corresponding number of negative responses. In every other item but one (High school acceptance of the middle school program), schools reporting negative outcomes amounted to fewer than 10% of respondents.

Table 2: Percentage of Positive and Negative Effects of Reorganization to Middle School.

Measure	Percent Positive	Percent Negative
Average daily attendance	46	3
Tardiness	34	
Truancy	49	6
Standardized test scores	36	5
Grade point average	54	3
Retentions in grade	51	3
Suspension rate	49	5
Expulsion rate	23	5
Discipline referral	54	8
School vandalism	46	
School theft	31	
Teacher/staff absenteeism	28	3
Teacher attrition	26	10
Articulation with elementary school	57	6
Parent conferences	67	
Race/ethnic relationships	26	3

Table 3 reports the perceptions of educators in "new" schools on the effects of reorganization in more subjective categories. Here, again, the outcomes are almost entirely positive, in all 24 categories. It is difficult to recall other educational innovations which have resulted in such strongly positive perceptions on the part of those involved. In the table below, the percentages listed in the column on the right are those reporting outcomes either strongly or moderately positive. Where negative outcomes were reported, they are identified in the second column. The remaining respondents indicated no effect of reorganization in these areas.

Table 3: Subjective Judgments About the Effectiveness of Middle Schools

Category	Percent Positive	Percent Negative
Student self-concept	82	
Student attitude toward school	82	
Student participation in special interest activities	79	
Student unruliness	49	5
Student physical health	26	
Student emotional health	57	
Student social development	69	
Teacher-staff confidence in managing disruptive students	67	3
Student confiednce in self-directed learning	59	
Teacher-staff morale	77	5
Teacher/staff attitude toward change	69	8
Teacher/staff rapport	72	5
Teacher/staff participation in special interest activities	69	3
Teacher/staff confidence in in student abilities	64	
Student creativity	62	
Teacher/staff variance in instructional strategies	72	3
Local media coverage of school programs	59	

TABLE 3 (CONTINUED)

Category	Percent Positive	Percent Negative
Parental support of school programs	75	
Community support of school programs	76	3
School board support of school programs	67	3
District office support of school programs	72	
High school staff perceptions of program success	47	16
Elementary school staff perceptions of program success	67	
Student feelings about teachers	77	

The outcomes associated with the transition to middle school undertaken by schools in the last five years, reported in Tables 2 and 3, were substantially positive, in every single category. Taken as a whole, the data indicated that when schools experienced changes in the above areas, (instead of reporting "no effect") those changes have been positive for almost every school. The outcomes are less positive, however, than those reported by the 1985 survey, also in almost every case. This may, we think, possibly have been due to the expansion of the sample to include more than middle schools identified as exemplary, and also because the schools in this portion of the 1993 sample included no schools older than five years.

Part Three of the 1993 survey asked respondents from "old" middle schools to identify the long term effects of middle school reorganization. Educators in schools which had been in operation for longer than five years were asked, first, to indicate whether certain program components had been an important part of their school. Then, respondents were asked to reflect on the causes related to the presence or absence of those programs, and to estimate the long term effects of the presence or absence of those programs on school outcomes. Twenty separate components were included in this part of the survey. The order in which the components appeared in the survey was intentionally designed so as not to reflect an order of priorities familiar to many middle school educators (beginning with block scheduling, including a question about the foreign language curriculum early in the list, etc.).

---

1. Flexible (perhaps block) scheduling in the master schedule has contributed to the long-term effectiveness of our middle school program.

73% Mostly Yes   18% Mostly No   9%   No Response

When respondents asserted that flexible scheduling had contributed (73%) to their long term effectiveness as a middle school, they identified several causes related to its importance in their school. Primary among those reasons was the empowerment which such a schedule delivered to teachers working in interdisciplinary teams. Respondents who were able to use flexible scheduling productively were also quick to point out that this component had been a part of their school program for a long time, and that it had been launched effectively only after substantial staff development associated with the design and use of the flexible schedule. Representative statements about why flexible scheduling had contributed significantly included these:

> *Teachers are empowered to develop strategies unique to their students.*

> *Move toward teacher empowerment has given teachers total control of instructional time.*

Have been able to try many things and restructure to better meet student needs.

Used school improvement to research idea and concluded teacher driven flexible schedule would enhance student learning.

Each team operates independently—schedule kids as they need to for their team.

Interdisciplinary teams empowered as small schools within a school.

Respondents claimed numerous positive effects that were attributable to their flexible schedule. Better understanding of the students and more interdisciplinary instruction and integrated curriculum were two such benefits. The flexible schedule was also seen as contributing to the presence of: heterogeneous grouping, better allocation of time for instructional needs, smoother transition from elementary school, elimination of bells, strong team "buy-in" for their decisions, increases in engaged learning time, positive bonding between teachers and students, and other factors. Most commonly, the flexible schedule was seen as a significant tool for transforming the school to the point where time became a servant of instruction, instead of the reverse.

Not all respondents reporting the presence of a flexible schedule were satisfied that it was being fully utilized in their schools. In some schools, the passage of years had transformed the opportunity to plan together into a "right" to two planning periods. Several reported that traditional secondary-oriented teachers had difficulty in utilizing the freedom and flexibility of the schedule. Others reported that it was easier to talk about changing the schedule than it was to accomplish it.

Respondents who reported that a flexible schedule had not been a part of their program (18%) identified mostly logistical problems which they perceived as having limited their ability to make the schedule more flexible. Sharing faculty with a high school, years of reductions in force, difficulties in accommodating mainstreaming, state music requirements, and school size were offered as reasons why flexible scheduling was not central to their school program.

The effects of their inability to create a flexible schedule included frustration of the part of teachers and administrators, unshakable rigidity in the use of time, resulting in a limit to the "ability to make major curriculum changes." Poor communication between curriculum areas, and poor curriculum alignment were also cited as the consequences of an inflexible schedule.

2. A real school philosophy widely shared by the staff based on the characteristics and needs of developing adolescents has contributed to the long-term success of our middle school program.

87% Mostly Yes   7%   Mostly No   6%   No Response

Respondents who reported positively did so with several causes in mind. Many reported that beginning with the vision for a school with the students in mind was what theologists might refer to as a "first cause." That is, nothing came before that. Furthermore, the philosophy came about as a result of intention and design, and from carefully designed staff development. The establishment of the middle school philosophy was serious business in these schools, not simply empty rhetoric or meaningless motions. Representative comments include these:

We based the design and development of our program on the needs and characteristics of the pre and early adolescent.

Our mission statement was developed when we opened and adjusted periodically.

We are in a school renewal program which enables us to revisit our beliefs and philosophy.

All teachers have taken the 'nature and needs of M. S. learner' through local staff development.

Our school was departmentalized in '84 and the staff had little knowledge of middle school concepts. The first thing done was to begin looking at the characteristics of our students.

We spend a lot of time talking about the unique characteristics of middle level kids.

The philosophy is constantly referred to in terms of our beliefs, values, and mission. We refer to our purpose even in casual discussions.

In spite of constant budget cuts, our staff still strives to meet student needs. Effort is based on experience and research with early adolescence.

As we adapt or revise the curriculum, we always affirm the teaching strategies and materials against the philosophy.

The effects of this philosophical commitment were varied. In some schools, the philosophy came into play in the hiring of new staff members. In others, it contributed to "better decisions, in terms of appropriateness." For some, it resulted in a more "child-centered school." Consensus was easier to reach in such schools, since " people know their personal agendas are not the top priority." School improvement, renewal, and change have emerged from using the philosophy as an evaluative tool. Change was easier to implement because "we have a shared belief system." Words like *focus, unity, ownership, student success,* and *consistency* appeared again and again in the reports from respondents where a strong school philosophy was at the center of school life.

When such a philosophy was not a part of the program, at least two factors seemed pertinent. One was that there was a "well-written philosophy on file rather than lived." The other factor seemed to relate to the ignorance of the staff of the unique characteristics of early adolescent learners, due to a preponderance of high school-oriented faculty on the staff. Ignorance of the learners' characteristics led to ignoring the characteristics in program design and implementation. The results of this were also clear: "junior high school;" "these people are slow to change;" and, "Sometimes we forget where we are going as a school in the community." Absence of a real school philosophy based on the characteristics and needs of the students robbed schools of their opportunity to "adopt a whatever it takes" posture toward the education of their students.

3. A foreign language program as an integral part of the curriculum has contributed to the long-term effectiveness of our middle school program.

43% Mostly Yes   45% Mostly No   10% No Response

Approximately equal groups of respondents answered *yes* or *no* to this question. Among those who reported a hardy foreign language program, many agreed that foreign language was in the middle school because of the presence of an "exploratory wheel" as a part of a unified arts curriculum. Others reported that it was present because of state department of education requirements. Schools where foreign language programs were described with some excitement and enthusiasm seemed to be those from higher socioeconomic status situations where strong college preparatory programs existed in the high school, or there was firm parent commitment to liberal arts curriculum, with the result that cast it in a very positive light in the community. In these schools, albeit only a few, students had the opportunity to study as many as four different languages: French, Spanish, Latin, and German.

At the time of the 1993 survey, it appeared that foreign language was not an influential part of the curriculum in most school programs.

4. A building and facilities designed especially for the middle school has contributed to the long-term effectiveness of our middle school program.

43% Mostly Yes   48% Mostly No   9%   No Response

Middle school leaders were not uniformly able to take advantage of buildings designed especially for a middle school program. Many programs inhabited old buildings, any number of which were built as long as 60 years before the middle school moved in. Most often these buildings were former high school or junior high school facilities, sometimes with adequate space but usually with classroom configurations which were less than facilitative of the interdisciplinary team organization. When it was possible to use the building to support the program, the effects frequently included the development of school-within-school designs, rooms organized by teams, and the facilitation of a more integrated curriculum. Even when the design of the building caused difficulties, many respondents appeared to have treated this as a challenge, and continued to find ways to implement middle school concepts effectively.

Those who found themselves able to utilize older facilities, included responses like these:

> *You cannot change a building; you can change the way you use it.*

> *Old building, but teaming works fine anywhere.*

> *Our school was originally a high school. The three floors design works well with separating our three grades.*

> *We have outgrown our building, and our school is effective despite the design.*

The large number of educators (48%) who felt blocked by the buildings in which their programs were placed, cited the departmentalized design of older secondary schools in which they were placed, and the various difficulties this raised for interdisciplinary teamwork as barriers. Teachers were unable to share adjoining classrooms, students rarely "saw themselves as a whole team," and science instruction suffered because of the difficulty in utilizing laboratories. Several respondents inhabited older "open space" facilities which still caused noise and other distractions; most of these facilities were under or scheduled to be under reconstruction to eliminate the open space. Others pointed to the difficulties they were experiencing with putting technology into older facilities.

5. A strong student recognition program provided through interdisciplinary teams has contributed to the long term effectiveness of our middle school program.

84% Mostly Yes   6% Mostly No   9% No Response

The schools in this survey reported recognition of students as being at the heart of their efforts. The very few who did not wrote that teams were non- existent at their school, and therefore student recognition was conducted on a school-wide basis; this, however, resulted in much less student recognition. Among those reporting a strong recognition program, these responses were typical:

> *Each of the nine interdisciplinary teams meet weekly to recognize students for achievement.*

> *We have a 9-week recognition program four times each year for students.*

> *Each core team recognizes each student during the school year.*

> *All teams have a budget and responsibility for student recognition.*

> *The school is divided into three houses, each with its own recognition program.*

> *Team student of the month, homework superstars, positive action kids, students in the art spotlight, and an awards assembly that recognizes participation as well as success.*

Large group meetings are held within the learning communities to recognize students academic achievement, efforts, and contributions to the community.

Since each house has its own funds, we are able to recognize many more student contributions than if it was done school-wide.

The results of such efforts are predictably positive. Students "feel good about themselves and their school." Interest in participating and doing well in both academic and nonacademic activities was high. Students were perceived as making extra efforts to meet various criteria for recognition. Students "feel special and connected to the school," with "better student esteem and a more positive attitude toward school." By recognizing students in these ways, " it helped to instill that 'proud and positive' attitude we strive for." The norm of positive recognition is ingrained in the school climate.

---

6. Flexible grouping strategies, primarily heterogeneous, have contributed to the long-term effectiveness of our middle school program.

85% Mostly Yes   12% Mostly No   3%   No Response

Educators in this sample of middle schools are strongly committed to flexibility in grouping as well as scheduling and other matters. In fact, to quote one principal, "The scout motto is 'Be Prepared.' The middle school motto is 'Be Flexible' !" While grouping was a part of many middle schools in this sample, the extent and rigidity of that grouping seemed far more limited than a random sample from the general population of middle schools might have indicated. Students in this sample often remained grouped for special programs for gifted and talented students, and grouping was also used frequently for mathematics and language arts. Just as often, however, efforts toward "inclusion" saw strenuous efforts to bring students with disabilities into the regular classroom, and heterogeneous grouping in every subject at every grade level. Cooperative learning featured heavily in both the causes and the effects of flexible grouping. Among those who reported flexibility in grouping were these comments about the causes of their grouping strategies:

> *Each interdisciplinary team is constructed to accurately represent the grade level composition.*
>
> *Master schedule permits flexibility in team planning and modifying instruction in subject areas.*
> *Have always been committed to heterogeneous grouping. Have a staff development initiative that equips our staff with a variety of instructional strategies for working with diverse groups.*
>
> *We continue to fight the small but powerful group of parents that want homogeneous grouping.*
> *In grades six and seven we have elementary trained teachers who adjust to student needs.*
>
> *Students acted like the labels they were given when tracked.*
>
> *Shared all the research. Discussion groups and then decision groups.*

*Block schedule, multiage configurations, and
proximity to other teams promotes flexible and
varied grouping patterns.*

The results of flexible grouping in their schools seemed to touch
on academic achievement, personal development, and group citizenship in the schools who reported.

*Everyone feels a part of school. There is no sense of
elitism. There is an atmosphere of 'can do' and
cooperation.*

Students in 6th grade rarely fail.

*Students have strong academic role models in each
of their classes, while others have the opportunity to
develop leadership roles in these same classes.*

*Teaching for learning for all is a common thread
that connects the [school] family. Teaching of
collaborative skills via cooperative learning has
decreased school-wide discipline problems.*

*Students work harder to do well, and teachers work
to better adapt instruction to meet students' needs.
A tremendous amount of teacher training has been
necessary to keep teachers from 'teaching down the
middle.' The new strategies are terrific for kids,
though.*

*Allows for more individualization and causes
students and teachers to work together more closely.*

The few respondents who reported that they were unable to utilize a flexible grouping strategy laid the responsibility for this on parent groups who worked for more rigid ability grouping, or curriculum mandates that made flexibility difficult to achieve. The results, one wrote, are a "discipline problem track and an AG [academically gifted] track." Even these respondents, however, seemed to recognize the desirability of moving to a more flexible grouping plan. "This has been extremely difficult due to pressure from parents who want specialized classes," one wrote. "However, the respondent continued, "we still continue to work on de-tracking."

---

7. A strong parent program that encourages both involvement and support for all parents has contributed to the long-term effectiveness of our middle school program.

68% Mostly Yes   25% Mostly No   7%   No Response

Since the early 80s, many school districts have placed a renewed emphasis on parent involvement in the schools. This accent on involvement is reflected in the survey responses. Formal parent advisory groups, site-based management, newly targeted communication efforts, official parent coordinator positions, regular parent visitation days, parent clubs, forums, and special classes—all of these devices, plus a new community importance placed on volunteerism, help to account for strong parent connections to many of the middle schools in this survey. In some schools the team organization was utilized so that each team had a program for parent involvement.

The results of positive parent involvement were worth the effort to respondents. Typical responses included these:

We are able to do things and make offerings that we couldn't without parent help.

Kids appreciate their parents' interest and involvement.

Parents play an active role in setting policy, assist in evaluation and employment of staff, and monitor all budgets.

Great support and interest in all aspects of our school program.

They serve on teacher hiring committees. Best hires!

Significant parent involvement is up to 27% from 1% in 1988.

A real sense of community exists at our school. Parents know how hard we all work to provide the best education.

Parents feel involved, connected, appreciated, and function as partners.

One of the contributing factors to our national recognition.

Happier parents who support the school; in turn,
happier students who are more effective learners.

Those respondents who were unable to report a strong parent program did so with reluctance. In most cases, it seemed that low parent involvement was tied to the socioeconomic status of the students attending the school. Parents worked several jobs, or lived miles from the school, or regular invitations sent home with students never seemed to get to the parents. The situation was certainly not preferred by the educators involved. The results were clear:

At times it is difficult to get community buy-in.

Many parents are not as informed on school issues
as they ought to be.

A PTA which is still operated by predominantly
affluent parents.

Lack of support by parents makes staff feel that
students are not being held to standards by parents.

Parents still complain about a less-than-welcoming
atmosphere.

---

8. An interdisciplinary team organization where teachers share students, space, and schedule, has contributed to the long-term effectiveness of our middle school program.

85% Mostly Yes   6% Mostly No   9% No Response

Few components of the middle school concept receive as much support from educators as does interdisciplinary team organization, and the respondents to this survey provided the same affirmation. Over and over, responses cited the belief that, from the first, interdisciplinary teams were considered at the heart of the school. The following responses were typical:

> *Part of the original organization of this school which has remained in place for 24 years.*

> *We had teaming from the first day.*

> *Set it up that way originally.*

> *Careful planning which listed this as nearly non-negotiable 12 years ago, and ongoing consultation with teachers to keep teaming vital.*

> *Critical. Team is the fundamental difference.*

Such commitments, plus common planning time, flexible schedules, proximity of team members' classrooms, supportive inservice education, created an effective learning environment for early adolescents. Respondents are enthusiastic about the results:

> *Team pride is acquired immediately by students and a positive climate is in evidence.*

> *Better planning by the team and better understanding of the students.*

An instructional climate that says whether what is learned is more important than when it is learned. We are truly continuous progress.

We have truly created eight communities within a school of 925 students. Students have a sense of identity.

Teachers are empowered. Parents see cooperative instructors. Students benefit from team instruction.

[Teams] provide a humanistic environment designed to meet the needs of all students. They are met each day by adults who like to teach, want them to learn, and know how to play.

Excellent academic progress.

Teacher help in leadership and management.

Innovative planning and integrated instruction. Students move from class to class with a minimum of disruption.

Nine small well-oiled units functioning within the whole.

In the few situations where teaming was not a critical component, it seemed to be related to the background and experience of the teachers. Teams might have functioned well in the sixth grades of a school, for example, but the seventh and eighth grades, in the same schools, were unable to do the same. Schedule, building, or curriculum difficulties combined with traditional secondary arrangements to make team organization less than it could be in the other schools. Again, the results are fairly well known at this point: less teacher communication; less student sense of community; less of most of the things that strong teams produce in the other schools.

9. Active instruction based on the learning styles of developing early adolescents has contributed to the long-term effectiveness of our middle school program.

66% Mostly Yes   25% Mostly No   7%   No Response

Schools where teachers are reported to be engaged in active learning opportunities for students often state that their recognition of the great diversity among early adolescents has propelled them into a struggle to find alternatives for classroom teaching. Virtually all of the respondents who indicated a commitment to active instruction described an equally intense commitment to staff development opportunities for teachers. Among the topics which were included in the staff development programs were: the nature of learning styles, cooperative learning, the reading/writing workshop approach, alternative assessment, mastery learning, hands-on activities, technology, integrated curriculum, multiple intelligence theories, and others. Also, bringing elementary certified teachers to the middle school seemed to almost automatically promote active learning. When teachers were able to invest their classrooms with more active learning based on the needs of early adolescents, good things happened:

Hands-on learning makes school come alive.

Better instruction and more successful learners.

Teachers are encouraged to try new ideas and told 'It's okay to fail' as they attempt to use new ideas with middle schoolers.

Active participation has decreased classroom referrals to the office.

Students are more actively involved and not turned off by 'sit and git' teaching styles.

Classrooms are busy and filled with cooperative learning. Our students perceive school as fun. Parents find education a positive thing. This has increased student self-esteem.

Majority of the students show marked academic progress as measured by standardized tests and teacher evaluations.

---

10. Articulating with high schools that have also developed programs based on aspects of the middle school concept (e.g., a high school that has begun or expressed interest in interdisciplinary teams, advisory groups, heterogeneous grouping, etc.) has contributed to the long-term effectiveness of our middle school program.

19% Mostly Yes   64% Mostly No   16% No Response

For most of the last two decades, middle level educators have reported that high school educators were generally critical and unsupportive, sometimes harshly so, of efforts to implement the middle school concept in place of the traditional junior high school (See the 1985 survey, for example). Respondents to the 1993 survey make it clear that, for at least some middle school educators, this is no longer the case. A new and fascinating mood of support for change has begun to appear, it seems, in many high schools. Many who were unable to respond "yes" to the above question, qualified their response by saying that such articulation opportunities had not been part of their "long term" experience, but that recently things have begun to change. Even among those who reported effective articulation with receiving high schools, it seems to have been a relatively recent phenomenon.

In some cases, respondents emphasized that attempts at closer articulation with high schools, in and of itself, was a new and pleasant experience for them and eventually for their students. Subject area meetings between eighth and ninth grade teachers were most common in this endeavor. Guidance departments in both settings have been actively collaborating to promote a smoother transition from middle level to high school. Several schools' reports indicated progress in this area.

In a number of other districts, middle level educators report an increasing implementation of middle school-style concepts at the high school level. This has begun to occur for a number of reasons:

Parents started complaining about the sterile and unfriendly atmosphere at the high school. At the same time, parents were praising the change process of the junior high to middle school.

*A former middle school principal moved to a high
school and added teaming last year.*

*Old ways die hard, but our program is forcing them
to change.*

*We have set up shadowing and department coordina-
tion as well as sharing students and teachers on our
campus. High school teachers are more and more
interested in what we are doing.*

*Our high school is just developing its readiness for
change and those ideas have been more widely
embraced when presented by another high school.*

*Because of the success at the middle schools with
interdisciplinary teaming, our feeder school has
begun to adopt our philosophy and train its staff.*

Kids got lost at the high school.

*Recent California high school reform recommends
all of the middle school programs mentioned in the
question.*

When high schools began to tailor their programs to the needs of
students, especially in ninth and tenth grades, several positive outcomes
were identified, albeit by a handful of respondents:

*It reduces dropouts and improves academic success
in subject areas.*

*Smoother transition. High school teachers are
becoming more child-centered.*

*Students and parents are more positive about the
transition from middle to high school.*

For the greater number of middle school educators, however, articulation with a high school organized with similar programs remained something to hope and work for rather than to celebrate. In some cases, respondents indicated that progress was being made; new energy was being devoted to restructuring the high school programs. In these situations, middle school educators are apprehensive but positive:

*The high school is investigating double blocked
periods and a rotating schedule for next year, on a
trial basis.*

*As we move to site-based management, 21st century
schools, etc., we see our high school beginning to do
team teaching, and an exciting Winter Intensive
Term that incorporates middle school ideas better
than we do! We are optimistic about the future.*

*The old high school principal was against middle
school because he got another grade level at the
high school. The new principal is very interested in
developing a transition team and looking at advisor-
advisee.*

Nonetheless, the majority of middle school educators reporting remained in situations where high school educators either ignored the reorganization of the middle level, or were openly hostile to it. Coordination between the two school levels was minimal. Different philosophies existed. In some cases, middle school educators believed that high school staff members were "threatened by the middle school movement." At best, the departmentalized organization and mindset of many high school teachers and administrators, respondents said, made it extremely difficult for them to see the value of interdisciplinary efforts. The result was that, often, high school educators viewed middle schools as "being too soft on kids, not getting them ready for high school."

11. A regular and systematic process for evaluating the middle school program has contributed to the long-term effectiveness of our middle school program.

71% Mostly Yes   19% Mostly No   9% No Response

A substantial majority of the schools responding to the survey were firmly committed to continuing evaluation of their school programs. Formal, frequent, systematic, and productive seemed to be adjectives that applied in many situations. In a number of schools, external models based on regional accreditation, state guidelines, effective schools research, or tools specific to the middle school concept were utilized. In others, site-based school improvement teams gathered data from standardized test scores, failure rates, parent concerns, student surveys, teachers' perspectives, local demographics, and recent research; these data then formed the basis for a careful evaluation of the school programs. Annual school goals were an important part of the process in many sites. The results of eliciting such efforts at feedback and guidance were clear:

The staff feels strongly that we know where we are and have established places for refinement.

A program that is continuously being updated and improved.

We change every year.

Student results and success rates are at the 95% level.

There's a strong feeling of pride in our school and a driving determination to continually improve and help our students.

We have made a tremendous amount of change (improvement) in a very short period of time.

Evaluation and goal setting cause us to be more focused and intentional in what we do in the class-room.

More credibility and staff support for the middle school concept.

We're constantly making a great school even better.

Some reporting schools, of course, were unable to mount or sustain a regular evaluation effort. It may not have been a high priority in the school or district. Others pointed to a lack of time, resources, or instruments. Others cited lack of a long-range plan which might serve as a background for evaluation. The results were negative:

Almost lost the middle school vision.

For three years no true evaluation has been done.

For five years there has been no critical analysis of why we are doing what we do. Main effect is we are slipping away from our mission.

Firm evidence of success is not available.

---

12. Team leaders that play an important role in school and teacher leadership have contributed to the long-term effectiveness of our middle school program.

81% Mostly Yes   10% Mostly No   9%   No Response

Teacher leaders were clearly an important part of the operation of the middle schools reporting in this survey. In several schools, this leadership was played out in "house" or departmental levels rather than on teams. Most schools, however, reported having an official school position of "team leader" for each interdisciplinary team in the school. However, a number of schools do not officially designate a team leader. Even in schools where team leaders are not officially chosen the responses indicated that regular teacher leadership was an important component of the effectiveness of the school. In some schools, team leaders were elected by team members; in others they were selected by the school administration. However they were identified, team leaders appeared to play two equally important roles in the reporting schools:

1) they were a critical part of the shared decision-making process at the school level; and 2) they acted as a "captain" of the team to which they belonged, guiding and supporting the work of the team in myriad ways. Respondents described the position of team leader as critically important to the mission of the middle school:

> *Team leaders are the lifeline of our teams.*

> *Team leaders are empowered to be leaders.*

> *Our team leaders are the cement of our school.*

> *Peer leadership is a strong way to begin new programs.*

In schools where team leaders played important parts in school governance, they usually did so as part of a school improvement council. Such councils met frequently, often weekly, to help establish the policies that lead to the implementation of school goals, to make decisions, and solve problems at the school level:

> *Team leaders are part of our school management team that addresses concerns of students, teachers, and parents.*

> *Team leaders meet as our Program Improvement Council weekly.*

> *The establishment of a strong leadership team based on a network of open communication helps everyone to play an active role in decision making.*

Teacher leadership is key in both the school improvement effort and house leadership.

Strong personalities often end up in middle schools. A school climate which likes transformational leadership creates more staff ownership of the total school program.

When teachers work closely with school leaders in these ways, the results are positive:

All staff members feel they are instructional leaders. This leads to more cooperation instead of competition. We are building a climate where we strive to challenge one another instead of just accepting each other.

Closer communications among faculty, staff, and administration. Full faculty cooperation, better teacher rapport within and outside of team groups.

A high degree of site-based management, teachers feeling they are professionals, good morale, improvements on an ongoing basis.

The team leader is the chief contributor to site-based management and overall climate of the school.

More efficient school operation, more committed teachers and teachers who contribute to the overall excellence of the system, as these teachers often assume system leadership roles.

Inside the team, the leaders facilitated the organization and operation of the learning experience for students, teachers, and parents. They also acted as a liaison between the team and the rest of the school. Team leaders "provide verbal and written communication and represent team members in decision-making activities." In such situations:

Our teams have become mini-families as the result of such effective leadership. Everyone is involved with team trips and team motivational projects.

Teams are cohesive, structured, organized, and involved...

Teachers listen to their peers because they are also in the trenches.

New programs develop; others are modified if needed; interdisciplinary units are created.

Only one school reported a negative experience in this area. The respondent asserted that "PIC became picky; they expect the principal to do it all."

---

13. A curriculum characterized by both a core academic focus and a broad range of exploratory activities has contributed to the long-term effectiveness of our middle school program.

73% Mostly Yes   12% Mostly No   13% No Response

Several years ago, James Garvin (1987) identified the expectations which parents had for middle level schools. Among those expectations were three which had direct implications for the design of a balanced curriculum: that students would find opportunities for success; that they would encounter a motivating program, and that they would receive appropriate preparation for high school. Respondents reported that they worked diligently to maintain a balance between a traditional core curriculum aimed at preparation for high school and an exploratory program aimed at stimulating interest in new areas and providing opportunities for students to experience success. Frequently, this meant that students engaged in what had come to be called a "wheel" of exploratory classes involving as many as a half dozen or more areas in the first year at the middle level, with some increasing specialization in the years that follow. Typically, a sixth grade student might have revolved through six different areas of the exploratory curriculum, choosing three of these for 12 weeks each the next year, and two for 18 weeks each the final year.

Middle school educators responding to this survey revealed a strong commitment to maintaining a motivating program for students, both in academic and exploratory areas. They also indicated a desire to unite academic and exploratory teachers in a common effort with equal importance. Although efforts were not uniformly successful, the results are frequently positive:

Students feel good about themselves and like school.

A living, changing program, with considerable willingness to try new ideas.

These (exploratory) courses got us started on our change to middle school and they have become the

*core of our program. Excellent teaching goes on
here. They are the model.*

*Exploratory teachers are teamed and are perceived
as important as academic teams.*

*We have designed our program based on kids'
development and needs rather than on available
staff and schedule.*

*Exploratory teachers feel a part of the team main-
stream.*

*We have changed constantly in our nine years.
Students and parents understand our focus and
acknowledge it. We do very well on system-wide
standard measures. Students have a great deal of
choice among electives.*

14. A smooth and continuous transition from elementary to middle school has contributed to the long-term effectiveness of our middle school program.

76% Mostly Yes   15% Mostly No   9% No Response

At least part of the original rationale for the middle school was the recognition that a smoother and continuous transition out of the elementary school was important to the effectiveness of the K-12 continuum. For many years, students leaving the elementary school and entering the junior high school were jarred by a unsettling clash between the cultures of the two educational levels. Even now, in many districts the transition is less than successful, with disruptions of one kind or another leading to increased numbers of students experiencing school failure as they move to the cusp of secondary education. For the most part, however, schools reporting in this survey have made remarkable progress in eliminating this problem.

Proximity and program congruence are clearly responsible for a substantial amount of transition improvement. Interestingly, those schools where one or two grades of the elementary school are housed on the middle school campus seemed to experience the smoothest transition. Also, schools where the fifth grade had traditionally been a part of the middle school experience reported few problems. Middle schools where the sixth grades were organized into two-teacher interdisciplinary teams also seemed to be able to provide a relatively smooth transition into the middle school. Team identity, itself, was also mentioned as an important component of the successful transition to middle school.

Well-designed and effectively implemented orientation and articulation programs were also a key component in this process. School counselors often appeared to take the leadership in these programs, but school administrators and teachers from both levels were frequently involved. Sometimes this was so thoroughly done that it resulted in weekly communications between schools at the two levels. Often many steps were involved: visits back and forth, videos, early orientations, newsletters, "buddy" and pen pal systems, workbooks, teacher-to-teacher talks, coffee meetings, and other elements are contained in what one respondent described as "a great articulation program with the elementary schools, one which is a continuing, on-going program, not a once-a-year program." With these elements in place, the transition experience was very different:

Little or no 'transition shock' for incoming students, identity with the team very strong, students more confident.

Fifth graders are comfortable with the middle school program before they get here.

Parents and students feel less apprehensive about the change and begin to feel excited about their move to the middle school.

Students move into the middle with little or no fear.

Sixth graders love our school.

Students who come from throughout the district are comfortable in a large school and develop coping skills during middle school. They are successful in high school.

---

15. A continuous program of staff development, renewal, and school improvement providing a steady stream of teachers and administrators trained and committed to educating the early adolescent has contributed to the long-term effectiveness of our middle school program.

62% Mostly Yes   28% Mostly No   10% No Response

Susan Rosenholtz (1989) argued that schools that were learning places for teachers are effective learning places for students. Teachers must, she wrote, be engaged in school and professional improvement before schools could offer the most productive experiences for their students. Schools where teachers did not grow, and did not participate in the decisions that effected their professional lives, may be places where student personal and academic growth was also stunted. The majority of respondents to the current survey offered evidence of their support of these arguments, identifying the source of their continued success as the continuous staff development programs they have mounted and maintained.

> *We believe that staff development is the key to an effective instructional program. Each year a significant amount of money is budgeted for staff development. This has resulted in teachers becoming and remaining excited about the move to middle school. The change from junior high school to middle school made us aware of all we needed to learn.*

> *We combine school improvement with ongoing inservice to better meet the needs of early adolescents.*

> *We are continually striving to upgrade our programs. We always seem to be on the cutting edge in pilot programs and inservice.*

> *We spend a lot of money and a lot of professional days on this, but it is the key to our success.*

> *We have not lost the 'middle school state of mind.'*

When this did not occur, it was often because of financial problems rather than the will to improve. Additionally, difficulties in some districts had, in recent years, compelled transfers of staff from the high school to the middle school, dramatically increasing the need for inservice education in a situation where staff development was the first item on the budget to be cut. The results were less than positive, usually involving a loss of momentum at the middle level school.

16. A shared decision-making model which is formal, systematic, and provides authentic collaboration between and among teachers, administrators, parents, and students has contributed to the long-term effectiveness of our middle school program.

73% Mostly Yes   15% Mostly No   12% No Response

It can be argued that the middle school concept and shared decision-making emerged onto the American educational scene at about the same time. Some would go so far as to say that middle school educators recognized and implemented shared decision-making before it became popularized with recent emphases on quality schools, school improvement, and similar models. It is certain that the majority of respondents to this survey attest to the value and utility of involvement and empowerment in this manner. In many middle schools, these procedures regularly involve teachers and administrators in collaborative efforts. There has been, according to these reports, much less success in regularly and effectively involving students, parents, and community members. When such a procedure was implemented effectively, the results are incontestably positive. Terms like *ownership, involvement, communication,* and *empowerment* were common in reports:

Joy in working together for a common purpose.

Decisions are more focused on teaching and learning. The decisions are better.

There's a cohesiveness, a sense of purpose, and things get done because we're in charge.

More of an ownership of events at school and community is apparent.

Teachers feel included and are more apt to internalize decisions.

Ownership, pride, and commitment.

---

17. An extracurricular program based on the needs of early adolescents, providing regular success experiences for all students has contributed to the long-term effectiveness of our middle school program.

72% Mostly Yes   15% Mostly No   13% No Response

One of the earliest and most rigorously pursued goals of the middle school movement was to eliminate what some called the "star system" in which a few students captured all the experiences and awards available at the school. Similarly, middle school educators have long argued for developmentally appropriate extracurricular activities wherein middle school activities would be matched to the characteristics and needs of early adolescents; this, instead of watered down versions of what they would encounter in high school in interscholastic athletics and social activities. Responses to the survey indicated that, for this limited sample, substantial progress had been achieved in these areas. Reasons stated include these:

Two intramural programs are in place, one in the mornings (required for all students) and an after-school program (optional).

Solid coaches and advisors who love kids and want middle school to work.

Age-appropriate socials, intramural sports, special interest exploratory programs.

Club meetings are held during the school day. Activity periods provide opportunity to join up to three clubs.
There is something for every student.

Only sports talented kids had opportunities to participate [earlier].

This has been a part of our program from the beginning. We examine it continuously.

We strive for 100% student participation.

Exploratory nature of students is reached. We offer everything from horseback riding to karate. Great for students.

Coaches have readily accepted middle school philosophy as being in the best interest of the child.

Once again, the results of these efforts are predictably positive: 'Student participation in our athletic program has probably doubled.'

Students, for the most part, are very happy to be at our school.

Almost all students find success in some extracurricular activity.

Our district's no-cut policy supports student participation.

Students who participate in this program feel more of an ownership in their school.

Parents and students feel students are getting a program that is comprehensive and meets individual needs of students.

Kids love playing without all the pressure of winning at all costs or being excluded from the team.

Of course, some schools reported that they had been unable to establish or maintain such programs. Among the factors cited as responsible for this failure are "cross bussing" which removed virtually all students from school grounds immediately after the end of the school day. Community expectations regarding interscholastic athletics were also cited. Others identified strong competition from community-based programs or lack of finances as the culprit. These respondents listed a diminution of school spirit, failure to "develop the loyalty they would in a true community school," "too much pressure on students to make the squad," and limited offerings as the consequence.

18. Interdisciplinary curriculum and instruction involving teachers from a variety of disciplines has contributed to the long-term effectiveness of our middle school program.

63% Mostly Yes   25% Mostly No   12% No Response

James Beane (1993) has argued persuasively that an integrated curriculum is the great unfinished business of middle level education. If so, the results of this survey indicated that many middle school educators were ready to complete that task. Clearly, the interdisciplinary organization of teachers was a necessary prerequisite to that work, and it has contributed mightily to the realization of the possibilities associated with an integrated curriculum. In such team arrangements, substantial progress appears to have been made toward the regular, if not frequent, planning and implementation of interdisciplinary thematic units, and the interest in "moving toward an integrated curriculum." Several respondents described the situation prior to these new directions:

> *The junior high teachers viewed this as the antithesis of good teaching.*
> *Teachers were only talking with teachers from the same discipline area. No curriculum connections or crossovers were made.*

When time, interest, skill, and opportunity are present and pulled together to make interdisciplinary and integrated curriculum possible, students experience a different sort of education:

Diverse viewpoints develop a program that has greater variety, vigor, and a broader perspective for meeting a wide range of student needs.

A holistic approach to learning, relates instruction to real life issues; when students 'do' they retain more, more self-directed learning takes place, breaking down the unnatural barriers of subject areas.

All students see the connection of curriculum topics and learn to work together.

Students can relate to how the exploratory program is connected to the academic program and how the different disciplines relate to each other.

We need to continue to work on this...but I think that this has had a direct positive impact on test scores.

Students see the real life aspects of their work, the quality of the work is better. It is an opportunity to provide varied instruction to mixed abilities.

Many middle schools were, however, far from providing integrated learning experiences for their students. Frequently, this was made difficult by lack of adequate training for staff members, traditional departmentalized preferences of teachers, lack of planning time, and the discouragement rising from the failure of initial poorly planned efforts.

19. Organizational arrangements which encourage long-term teacher-student relationships (e.g., multiage grouping, student-teacher progression, school-within-school) has contributed to the long-term effectiveness of our middle school program.

30% Mostly Yes   58% Mostly No   12% No Response

Few middle schools in this study reported organizational structure, of the type listed as examples, which encouraged or permitted long term teacher-student relationships. In those schools reporting the presence of such arrangements, most described other avenues for developing strong teacher-student relationships. Many, for example, referred to advisory programs which kept the same group of students together, with one teacher-advisor, for up to three years. A number of schools were organized so that counselors and even administrators moved with the students for three years. Others pointed out that this existed in exploratory or special education programs but not in general education. Still others interpreted the "school-within-school" program to mean grade level interdisciplinary teams where sixth, seventh, and eighth graders were housed in separate parts of the school building. The presence of these arrangements was, perhaps, so rare, that the question may have been misunderstood by a number of respondents.

Those schools who did report such arrangements, however, reported real benefits in relationships within the school. Close relationships between advisors, students, and parents developed over a period of several years. A greater sense of "family" grew in the school. Teachers came to know their students so well that benefits accrued in a number of areas: discipline, diagnosis of student learning needs, curriculum adaptations, accurate identification and placement of students in special programs, and others. We continue to believe that, as a sense of community continues to disintegrate in the lives of students outside the school, such a sense of belonging becomes even more important inside the school. To date, however, there is only the most meager evidence that these practices are recognized as potentially important aspects of middle school education.

20. A teacher-based guidance, advisory program has contributed to the long-term effectiveness of our program.

54% Mostly Yes   31% Mostly No   12% No Response

Responses to this item indicated a wide divergence between theory and practice in this area of middle school education. The advisory function of the middle grades teacher seems to have had great appeal as a concept, but educators have encountered great difficulty when attempting to implement the program and maintain it over a long period of time. Many who implemented the program found that teachers often resisted assuming the role of advisor, parents sometimes misunderstood the purpose of the program, the energy required to maintain the program was difficult to sustain, and "pressure for high performance in state examinations" caused the time for the program to be usurped by other needs. This component of middle level education, though often implemented in middle schools, has often failed to be sustained over the years:

We have not done this well, although we have tried several things over the years.

This has been the most difficult aspect of the middle level concept to implement.

The program was tried early, but died because of a lack of teacher support and administrative guts.

We have AA's. Some are super; others exist.

An advisory program is in place, but it only meets once a month.

We do not believe that a 'forced' advisory program is as effective as the natural relationships that develop in our loose plan.

We would like to move in the direction of teacher-based guidance but contractual language needs to be changed.

I don't think this program has had the kind of impact advertised in middle school journals.

Successful programs do exist, however, in many reporting schools. These programs, respondents claim, resulted from hard work and careful planning:

Good initial planning and considerable system and site-based efforts to keep advisor-advisee program strong.

There is an organized, planned advisory program in our school. Teams plan their programs based on student needs.

We developed an advisory curriculum and resource materials for teacher support. We provided inservice and hired an advisory program coordinator. Administrators and counselors had advisory groups and the program changed at each grade level, based on developmental differences in students. The program has an ideal combination of design, structure, and flexibility.

Under these circumstances, the results are positive:

Most students feel that they have a mentor/teacher they can confide in. Homeroom is a comfortable, safe place.
Most students feel safe and cared-for here.

Teachers get to know their students in a different dimension from the academic class.

These groups all foster personal/social growth and teach students how to work and learn together productively. ❏

SUMMARY AND CONCLUSIONS: THE 1993 STUDY

❏ The majority of middle schools reporting indicated that they have implemented most of components included in the middle school concept.

❏ Schools that have maintained the middle school concept for an average of ten years indicated that several components contributed a great deal to the long-term effectiveness of their program. In particular, the interdisciplinary organization of teachers appeared to be the central component of reporting schools, both "new" and "old." Along with, or as a part of the interdisciplinary team organization, several other components contributed to the effectiveness of middle schools: team leaders, flexible scheduling, student recognition programs, shared decision-making, heterogeneous grouping, and a student-centered school philosophy.

❏ Foreign language programs, organizational arrangements encouraging long-term teacher-student relationships, advisor-advisee programs, school buildings designed for middle school concepts, and effective relationships with receiving high schools have been less than central to the long-term effectiveness of middle schools identified as exemplary.

❏   When implemented effectively, the middle school
     concept increasingly leads to substantially positive
     outcomes in virtually every area of concern to educators
     and parents, including academic achievement. Improve-
     ment can also be noted in a range of aspects of student
     deportment, such as attendance, tardiness, referrals to the
     office for discipline, theft, vandalism, etc. Middle
     school programs improved relationships between:
     students of different racial and ethnic groups; parents
     and teachers; teachers and students; and, teachers with
     other teachers, especially between elementary, high
     school, and those at the middle level.

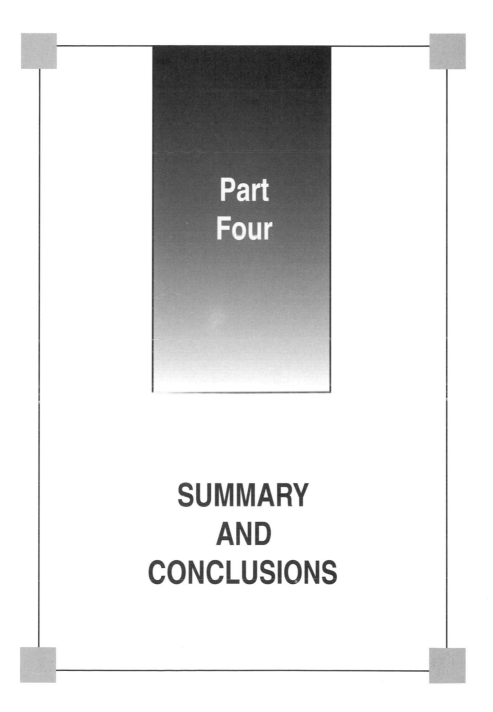

Part
Four

SUMMARY
AND
CONCLUSIONS

T he first part of the contemporary period of middle school education, from the early 60s, was a time when experimentation and innovation began to bring clarity and definition to the middle school concept. During this period of the 60s and 70s, research efforts were largely unproductive, prematurely emphasizing holistic comparisons between schools named "middle" and those with the name "junior high." Researchers presumed that differences in school name, grade level, or even vague differences in stated philosophy might be reflected in outcomes such as academic achievement at the school level. Some research efforts may have been conducted by opponents of the new middle level schools, motivated by a desire to demonstrate that no substantial improvements accompanied the appearance of middle schools. As we now know, many if not most middle schools were established for reasons which had little to do with student academic or developmental outcomes. New middle schools appeared because they facilitated court-ordered school desegregation plans, helped solve school building dilemmas, or eased school district student population difficulties. Little wonder that such priorities were not translated through training into measurable differences in school organization and outcomes such as academic achievement. In spite of a continuing disappointment in the outcomes of this sort of research, educators persisted in their efforts to implement a school focused on the needs of early adolescence, regardless of the external factors which may have brought it into existence.

During the 1970s and early 1980s, educators struggled toward consensus on the central elements of exemplary middle schools. The number of years which were required to achieve such a consensus indicates the complexity and difficulty of doing so. Implementation of these components was, at this formative time, understandably not as consistent, widespread, or effective as its proponents would have preferred. Detractors continued to point to the inability of middle school educators to identify demonstrably superior outcomes. Research comparing early versions of the middle school with the traditional junior high school continued to be largely unproductive. By the mid-1980s, however, a substantial national consensus had been reached concerning the fundamental elements of the exemplary middle school. It is likely that this consensus was formed at least in part because practitioners increasingly identified positive outcomes associated with the effective implementation of the components which eventually became the center of the middle school concept.

Recent evidence suggests that, from this consensus, middle school educators have moved, in the 80s and 90s, to implement recommended programs with increasing frequency and effectiveness. albeit still in a minority of middle level schools nationally. The interdisciplinary organization of teachers and students has begun to replace the high school and university style subject-centered academic departments. Flexible scheduling facilitates such organization in more and more schools, and flexible (primary heterogeneous) grouping arrangements tend to accompany the teams and their schedules. Middle school educators continue to insist that all students in the school are equally valuable and deserve an equitable education. Consequently, increased efforts to recognize and reinforce all students have followed the prerequisite effort to downplay old forms and programs which resulted in what some have called a "star system" where only a few students received school recognition. A new appreciation of the need for an integrated curriculum appears to be emerging from the earlier successes with interdisciplinary team organization. In fact, we would argue that it was necessary for teachers to work together in such teams before they could recognize or implement a truly integrated curriculum. Middle school teachers continue to try to find ways to implement more active teaching and learning experiences in their classes. Many educators also continue to struggle to find the correct format and curriculum for teacher-based advisory programs. Shared decision-making increases—along with other components distinguishing successful middle schools from their predecessors.

Accumulating evidence suggests that, when the essential elements of an exemplary middle school are thoroughly and effectively implemented, the outcomes are almost always positive. We suggest that research conducted in situations in which the effective implementation of required components can be documented will increasingly reflect the desired outcomes of middle school education: increased academic achievement, more wholesome personal development, and more positive group citizenship.

In the last three decades, the middle school movement has gained increasing momentum, in a period when other educational innovations became less viable, disappeared, or became increasingly conservative in nature. The continued existence of the middle school concept and movement is an exception to the rule. That the process has resulted in greater and greater national presence and validation is truly exceptional in the history of American education. With the possible exceptions of the Progressive Education movement, which in many aspects is the parent of the current middle school movement, and the century-old school consolidation process, no educational reorganization has affected so many teachers, students, parents, and communities.

This is not to say that we can declare the middle school movement an unqualified success with a guaranteed future. In hundreds, perhaps thousands, of schools called "middle," the components of the program are honored more in the breach than in their presence. In such schools, teams exist in organization but not in action. Advisory programs are merely seemingly endless 30-minute homerooms. The curriculum parallels what the Committee of Ten recommended a century ago. Instruction can often be even more traditional than the curriculum. More tragically, middle schools which had been models of effective programs have all too often experienced "educational erosion" resulting in the disappearance of exciting and empowering educational experiences.

Thornton Wilder once wrote that "Every good and excellent thing stands moment by moment on the razor's edge of danger and must be fought for." **We believe that the available evidence suggests that practitioners can, with confidence, continue to expect the implementation of middle schools to result in improved academic achievement, more positive personal development, and enhanced group citizenship for the students involved. But it isn't guaranteed, and it won't be easy.** ❏

REFERENCES

Alexander, W. M. (1968). *A survey of organizational patterns of reorganized middle schools: Final report, USOE project, 7-D-026.* Gainesville, FL: University of Florida.

Alexander, W.M. & George, P.S. (1993). *The exemplary middle school. 2nd Edition.* New York: Holt, Rinehart and Winston.

Alexander, W. M. & McEwin, K. (1989). *Schools in the middle: Status and progress.* Columbus, OH: National Middle School Association.

Barris, N. (1992). A comparative study of the Michigan Educational Assessment Program results between selected traditional junior high schools and middle schools in the state of Michigan to determine the organizational structure in which grade 7 students are most successful. *Dissertation Abstracts International, 54,* 34-A.

Beane, J. (1993). *A middle school curriculum: From rhetoric to reality, Second Edition.* Columbus, OH: National Middle School Association.

Bedford, R. (1993). *Middle level education survey. Report of results.* Patchogue, NY: Suffolk County BOCES.

Bryan, T. The relationship of eighth grade achievement scores and type of middle grades experience. *Dissertation Abstracts International, 48,* 2200-A

Carnegie Council on Adolescent Development (1989). *Turning points: Preparing youth for the 21st century.* New York: The Carnegie Corporation of New York.

Cawelti, G. (1989). *Middle schools a better match for early adolescent needs, ASCD survey finds.* Washington, DC: Association for Supervisions and Curriculum Development.

Clay, D. (1992). A comparison of junior high schools to middle schools with respect to achievement and attendance. *Dissertation Abstracts International, 53,* 1117.

Coleman, J. (1966). *Equality of educational opportunity.* Washington, DC: U.S. Government Printing Office.

Connors, N. & Gill, J. (1991). Middle schoolness and the federal school recognition program. *T.E.A.M.: The Early Adolescent Magazine, 4,* March/April, 44-48.

Council of Chief State School Officers (1992). *Turning points: States in action.* Washington, DC: Council of Chief State School Officers.

Damico, S. (1982). The impact of school organization on interracial contact among students. *Journal of Educational Equity and Leadership, 2,* 238-52.

Dirks, R. (1992). Middle level education: Its implications for the at-risk student(dropouts). *Dissertation Abstracts International, 52,* 3812-A

Doda, N.M. (1983, March). Middle school organization and teacher world view. Paper presented at the meeting of the American Educational Research Association, New York City.

Doda, N.M. (1984). Teacher perspectives and practices in two organizationally different middle schools (Doctoral dissertation, University of Florida, 1984). *Dissertation Abstracts International, 45,* 3058-A.

Doran, M. (1989). Socialization and achievement of students in a newly-implemented middle school. *Dissertation Abstracts International, 50,* 2322-A.

Dorman. G. (1983). Making schools work for young adolescents. *Educational Horizons. 61,* 175-82.

Epstein, J. L. & Mac Iver, D. J. (1990). *Education in the middle grades: National practices and trends.* Columbus: National Middle School Association.

Ernest, K. (1991). Effectiveness of an interdisciplinary team teaching organization on student achievement and student attitudes toward school in selected middle schools. *Dissertation Abstracts International, 52,* 2492-A.

Ferrara, R. (1993). a program evaluation of interdisciplinary team teaching in a suburban Northern California middle school. *Dissertation Abstracts International, 54,* 2007-A.

Garvin, J. (1987). What do parents expect from middle level schools? *Middle School Journal, 19,* 3-4.

George, P. (1983). *The theory z school.* Columbus, OH: National Middle School Association.

George, P. (1975). Ten years of open space schools: A review of the research. Gainesville, FL: The Florida Educational Research and Development Council. *Research Bulletin.*

George, P. & Oldaker, L. (1985). *Evidence for the middle school.* Columbus: National Middle School Association.

Georgia Board of Education (1993). *Linking services for Georgia's young adolescents.* Atlanta: Georgia Board of Education.

Hall, L. (1993). Effectiveness of interdisciplinary team organizational pattern of one half of a seventh-grade class compared with traditional departmentalized pattern of the other half of a seventh grade of a selected American middle school in Europe. *Dissertation Abstracts International, 54,* 1215-A.

Johnston, J.H. (1984). A synthesis of research findings on middle level education. In J.H. Lounsbury (Ed.), *Perspectives: middle school education, 1964-1984.* Columbus, Ohio: National Middle School Association.

Klingele, W.E. (1985). Is the middle school just an educational fad? Concerns of a teacher educator. *Middle School Journal, 16, (2),* 14-15.

Lawrence, C. (1989). A study of eighth-grade student performance into school organizational patterns. *Dissertation Abstracts International, 50,* 111-A.

Lee, V. & Smith, J. (1993). Effects of school restructuring on the achievement and engagement of middle grade students. *Sociology of Education, 66,* pp. 164-187.

Levine, D.E. Levine, R.F., & Eubanks, E. (1984). Characteristics of effective inner-city intermediate schools. *Phi Delta Kappan, 65,* 707-11.

Lewis, A. C. (1993). *Changing the odds: Middle school reform in progress, 1991-1993.* New York: Edna McConnell Clark Foundation.

Lipsitz, J. (1984). *Successful schools for young adolescents.* New Brunswick, NJ: Transaction Books.

Lipsitz, J. (n.d.). *Successful schools for young adolescents: a summary.* Carrboro, NC: The Center for Early Adolescence.

Lounsbury, J. & Clark, D. (1990). *Inside grade 8: From apathy to excitement.* Reston, VA: National Association of Secondary School Principals.

Lounsbury, J. & Johnston, H. (1988). *Life in the three sixth grades.* Reston, VA: National Association of Secondary School Principals.

McEwin, C. K. & Clay, R. (1983). *Middle level education in the United States: a national comparative study of practices and programs of middle and junior high schools.* Boone, NC: Appalachian State University.

McGrath, T. J. (1991). The associations between students' perceptions of school attitudes(school climate). *Dissertation Abstracts International, 52,* 1597-A.

McPartland, J. (April, 1991). How departmentalized staffing and interdisciplinary teaming combine for effects on middle grades students. Paper presented at the Annual Conference of the American Educational Research Association, Chicago, IL.

Myers, R. (1988). A comparison of academic achievement of middle schools and junior high schools on the Idaho proficiency examination and Iowa test of basic skills. *Dissertation Abstracts International, 49,* 3607-A.

National Institute for Education. (1983). *A study of the demography of schools for early adolescence.* January 1981. Washington, DC: U.S.D.O.E. Statistical Information Office.

Pinegar, D. (1991). A cross-sectional investigation of academic and affective differences related to junior high school or middle school experiences(academic differences). *Dissertation Abstracts International, 52,* 873-A.

Ritzenthaler, B. (1993). An investigation of key programs and practices of the middle school concept in institutionalized and non institutionalized middle schools in Florida. *Dissertation Abstracts International, 54,* 2535-A.

Rosenholtz, S. (1989). *Teachers' workplace.* New York: Longman.

Rosenshine, B. & Stevens, R. (1986). Teaching functions. In Wittrock, M. *Handbook of research on teaching, 3rd edition,* pp. 376-391. New York: Macmillan.

Rutter, M., Maughan, B., Mortimore, P., Ouston, J., & Smith, A. (1979). *Fifteen thousand hours: secondary schools and their effects on children.* Cambridge, MA: Harvard University Press.

Slavin, R., Ed. (1989). *School and classroom organization.* Hillsdale, NJ: Lawrence Erlbaum Associates.

Venerable, L. (1993). The perceived implementation of the essential characteristics of middle level education in Arizona's schools. *Dissertation Abstracts International, 54,* 2424-A.

Warren, L. (1993). Middle grades organizational patterns and their relationship to students' self concepts and perceptions of their school climate and teachers' efficacy and perceptions of their working environment. *Dissertation Abstracts International, 54,* 2112-A.

Wayson, W.W., DeVoss, G.G. Kaeser, S.C., Lasley, T., Pinnell, S.S., & the Phi Delta Kappa Commission on Discipline. (1982). *Handbook for developing schools with good discipline.* Bloomington, IN: Phi Delta Kappa.

Will, G. (1994). "Facing the great education debate," *Gainesville Sun,* February 17, p. 12-A.

Worley, M. T. (1992). A comparative study of change in middle level school organization: Middle school or junior high school? *Dissertation Abstracts International, 53,* 2611-A.